IN THE FIELD

Palimpsest Press
1171 Eastlawn Ave.
Windsor, Ontario. N8S 3J1
www.palimpsestpress.ca

Printed and bound in Canada
Cover design and book typography by Ellie Hastings
Edited by Jim Johnstone

Palimpsest Press would like to thank the Canada Council for the Arts and the Ontario Arts Council for their support of our publishing program. We also acknowledge the assistance of the Government of Ontario through the Ontario Book Publishing Tax Credit.

Canada Council for the Arts
Conseil des Arts du Canada

Canadä

LIBRARY AND ARCHIVES CANADA CATALOGUING IN PUBLICATION

TITLE: In the field / Sadiqa de Meijer.
NAMES: De Meijer, Sadiqa, 1977- author.
IDENTIFIERS: Canadiana (print) 20250245248
Canadiana (ebook) 20250247720

ISBN 9781990293993 (SOFTCOVER)
ISBN 9781997508007 (EPUB)
SUBJECTS: LCGFT: Essays.
CLASSIFICATION: LCC PS8607.E4822 I5 2025 | DDC C814/.6—DC23

IN THE FIELD

SADIQA DE MEIJER

CONTENTS

Liefhebben en nieuwsgierig zijn;
daartussen slaapt een zachte lijn.

—Leo Vroman

Loving and being curious;
between the two a soft line rests.

FOUND

I lost my notebook.

This was, for a few days that summer, my distracted answer when people asked me how I was.

It clearly wasn't a disaster, I wanted to convince myself, but my body seemed to argue; there was a void in my chest, and I couldn't relax, repeating my searches until they were senseless compulsions.

Only some of that discomfort had to do with the possibility of exposure—that someone, anyone, might read my private scribblings. Sure, it was unsettling to imagine eye contact with that individual, to be so inwardly naked, but after those seconds of awkwardness, I would have my notebook back. The universe would resume its semblance of order.

First, it wasn't in the three likeliest places. Not in my pocket, or in the maroon messenger bag, or on my desk. Then it wasn't in other bags either, or on the table, or in the corner of the living room where books tended to cluster. Not on the shelf by the phone, or the kitchen counter, or my dresser.

I searched every notebook-sized vacancy in our home: between the couch and its cushions, between furniture and walls, inside the furnace vents, among the toys.

Interrogating the three-year-old, trying to sound unconcerned. Did you play with it? Did you hide it?

It wasn't in the alley between my locked bike and the door. Not on the sidewalks or in the gutters along recent routes of travel. And not in the sand of the playground, or in the grassy parking lot of the farm where I last wrote in it, or in the lost and found of the art gallery where I thought I had felt its weight in my pocket.

As I searched the neighbourhood, I found other things: a broken phone, a working MP3 player (mostly Beatles songs), a child's shoe, a credit card, a ring, scraps of shopping lists (grapefruit, razors) and study notes (pulmonary physiology). I put up posters with the notebook's likeness. MISSING, REWARD. As I fastened them to buildings and lamp posts, neighbours and strangers commiserated. They told me of other, worse writerly losses: a car stolen with a handwritten poetry manuscript on the passenger seat, a novel on a computer in a room that flooded. Someone wrote *I hope and pray that you find it* on the poster in the grocery store.

The days were swept with rain. If the notebook was outside, it was probably soaked. Maybe the ink of my name and phone number had blotted illegibly. Maybe the pages had come loose under the wheels of cars and trucks. Or maybe it was inside the house and remained jammed in an unlikely corner, steps from where I slept.

And what was in it?

Things I thought or saw or overheard—whatever seemed to matter, even though I couldn't yet say why. Almost a year's worth of writing, from minute cursive paragraphs to large, hurried scrawls.

There were notes from lectures and other events—the idea of a reader feeling comfortable rather than spellbound within a work, a series of viewer responses to a friend's paintings.

A sight I walked past with my daughter one day: a man in a hard hat emerged from a house and started vomiting on the front lawn and between each heave took one long drag from his cigarette.

Something I overheard while at that farm, where we were picking strawberries: a jolly, elderly woman saying, I'm covered in bug juice, the good stuff with lots of DEET! I liked the words bug juice. I thought it was odd to praise DEET and organic berries in almost the same breath.

Serial attempts at describing the sound of pigeons cooing. Names of movies to see and books to read. How I felt in the hour before reuniting with a favourite teacher after almost two decades. The sight of a woman walking with an ornate wooden crucifix on her shoulder, pausing to wink at me.

The unliterary, too: a recipe for yogurt, shopping lists, private intentions and admonitions, phone numbers, tasks.

And small drawings done for or by my daughter—granting her my notebook usually gave me a few minutes of quiet. The progression in her forms over that year: from waving lines to rudimentary faces. My records of short conversations with her, the peculiar or endearing or funny statements I wanted to remember.

I was doing the work of looking after her, along with working several part-time jobs. I wasn't sleeping enough or reading enough, and often it felt impossible to have an uninterrupted thought. I don't mean to overstate the difficulty; I could have written, I suppose, or someone in my circumstances could have written—but I didn't. Those years held bright and profound experiences, and they also made me feel that I might prove to be a writer only in my mind. My notebook, then, was the small but reliable dwelling where my potential self could live.

When I was a teenager, my mother found a poster on the curb on garbage day and gave it to me.

An image mounted on foam board. I live with it still. The board is as tall as my waist, but before I went upstairs to take its measure, I wrote that it reaches my chest; my mind inflating the dimensions with meaning.

The poster advertises a long-gone exhibition at the Rijksmuseum in Amsterdam titled *Millet & Van Gogh*. The text and background are an electric red and blue and leave a vivid retinal imprint. Within them, the deep vista and muted tones of Millet's well-known painting, *The Gleaners*.

We had been in Canada for a nebulous length of time: too briefly for either of my parents to have secure employment, but long enough to feel a diminishing of the relationships with everyone we'd left behind. A phase of shifting our weight, leaning more heavily on the new map. I was close to leaving home. I wanted to study art, and my father was violently against it. We fought until I gave in.

The neighbourhood south of the Rijksmuseum is where I was born, on a short street named for Millet. The poster, when my mother found it, was a beacon that lay both far behind and out in front of me.

The women in the painting glean; they gather what the harvesters have missed. One has lifted the bottom of her apron and tied its corners to make a pocket. Each woman holds a small bundle of grain, which won't be enough to sell, but is for their private use.

In *The Gleaners and I*, Agnes Varda follows contemporary French gleaners, who still pick the potatoes and grapes and apples left after the harvests, and urban gleaners who gather food and other items from dumpsters or on the grounds of farmers' markets. Near the film's end, Varda acknowledges the metaphoric gleaning she does with her camera, picking images from the field of visual possibilities. Watching that documentary in the summer of the missing notebook, I saw that what I'd lost was a gleanings container.

Later, in the wake of the film, the metaphor settled in deeper. Leaving home, when home is a place that hurts, leads to the slow and strange revelation that the outside world is friendlier than the family that made you. It took me a long time, living in many rooms and apartments, to trust that most days of my life would pass without disparagements or threats.

I was gleaning not only as an aspiring writer, but also as a mother. Every day, feeling my own childhood pass through me almost too viscerally, I had to find what was worth saving from the stubbled field. To glean from farms or garbage is a method of survival. Gleaning from life might be as consequential; here are the grains I choose to take and plant again.

I started a new notebook. My notes on Varda's film are in it. Tasks from a meeting of the parent committee at school. A short list of plants that grow in the trampled parts of the park: plantain, dandelion, clover.

A friend's phrase: *I'm moonlighting as a trauma surgeon.*

A list of subversive answers to the question *where are you from?*

Email addresses and phone numbers, some without any context I can recall.

The words CLOSE THIRD PERSON! taking up a whole page.

A stern note to read Darwin.

The dimensions of our front window.

Lists of slant rhymes: panic/tonic, detector/doctored, elder/alder.

Occasionally, I remember something I've written down—the vague return of a thought or idea with promise in it—and flip through the pages. When I realize this material is in the old, lost notebook, there's a small ache, and a flaring of *maybe*, maybe it will still return to me.

My daughter is at the stage now of pretending to write. I give her my new notebook, flatten it open. Her attempts at script consist of strings of loops, like a stretched old-fashioned telephone cord. She concentrates, her brow furrowed, and beams over the results. So the first writing is recursive; momentarily, it tricks the endless forward line and circles back, hovers protectively over the present, then makes a loop that can hold it.

BLOODWORK

Every culture has its rituals for making healers. The August sunlight moves like a tide over the stone walls of campus, mosaics trees into a thousand greens, bursts from the side mirror of a rental truck. We sweat and wait in a hesitantly conversational lineup for name tags. Play children's games on the park's shorn grass. View bottled organs at a museum, their parts pinned with labels of typewriter text. Shout into one another's ears at thumping bars.

One hundred new medical students, placing their stethoscope orders. Over and over, we tell each other what we studied and where. Some people's biographical sketches begin to circulate: there's a neuroscientist enrolled in a concurrent doctoral degree, an engineer who also plays varsity women's hockey, a soldier whose tuition is covered by the military, after which he'll owe five years of service. I hear of someone claiming to have studied the year 1826. Other distinctions include being over thirty or having children.

My feeling of dwelling at the group's edge is both accurate and inflated: I have poetry on my mind, and a scavenged rose strung through my backpack, but I'm not the only one whose parents clipped grocery coupons or who listens to PJ Harvey or was on the waitlist before receiving an acceptance. That call came and I tried to start over. Threw out my notebooks, gave paint and canvases away. I meant to eliminate their distraction. It felt like a solemn and terrible thing to do. I hadn't read or heard James Baldwin yet—his absolving words: *it is not your fault, it is not my fault, that I write.*

We tour the new teaching facility, where the simulated clinic rooms have one-way mirrored walls, and plastic wrap still covers the examination tables. The building is named for the pharmaceutical company that funded its construction. I raise my hand to say this is ethically objectionable. Between that and wearing a Food Not Bombs T-shirt, I find that my biography circulates as well.

Our class has a single Indigenous student, who is soon rumoured to have been admitted for that reason. No one openly identifies as queer. We're told repeatedly during welcome speeches that we are the first cohort in the school's history with a female majority. It's not just a brotherhood anymore, croaks one emeritus.

None of the speeches mention that it has been less than forty years since the medical school lifted its prohibition against Black students. The only one in our class has a British and a Jamaican parent; later, he and I will trade stories of being halfbreeds. This right to use the slur as shorthand for our experience—it tastes faintly bitter to me, and comforting as well, like the blend of mustard leaves and cream in the saag that awaits in my freezer, cooked by my father. He wanted to be a doctor himself.

The classmate is very funny. For his birthday, I'll stitch *laughter is the best medicine* onto a pair of gloves. The faculty's motto is *Manu et Corde Medicus*, doctor in hands and heart, and I like the sound of that, skilled gestures made from a core of feeling.

On the third day, the class gathers in an amphitheatre of stone steps. We're there to recite the Hippocratic Oath, standing shoulder to shoulder in blindingly white half-coats. Smells of starched fabric and humid lake air. The History of Medicine professor reads out lines that we repeat in chorus. When the part comes that vows against giving a woman a pessary to induce abortion, I'm relieved to hear pockets of silence to match my own.

We're on the threshold of a process, collective and solitary, where others cannot follow. All of us have studied organic molecules. Our new medium will be bodies, first the dead, and then the vulnerable, unruly living. Their spleens, the rashes on their shins, their questions about insomnia.

But it's early, and I'm learning names: L. has peaked eyebrows, is vegetarian, and studied genetics, and K. shakes my hand with vigour, worked at the Royal Ontario Museum, and asks how tall I am. I meet the history major; he was making that up about 1826. Blond hair, shrewd eyes behind frameless glasses. He asks what kind of doctor I want to be, and I hear myself say that I'm a writer and am only gathering material. What is that strange chemistry we have with certain people, causing us to land inside ourselves with a thud? My face is suddenly warm—I've published a handful of pieces, quietly, without telling anyone—but he takes the comment as the joke I thought it was.

There's a barbeque at the Dean's house. Bringing swimwear is encouraged. This shift to undressing snags somewhere in my mind. Half a year earlier, in the city of my undergraduate degree, I bought my first and only suit. It was necessary, I'd been told by a medical student, the boyfriend of an acquaintance; there was no other way to dress for the interview. I knew the change rooms of every thrift store in that city, often trying on items for their singularity alone: sequined sweaters with feathers, a white jumpsuit of paper-like material, a vinyl skirt so stiff it stood upright. But when I pulled on the suit, the mirrored image at Reitmans or Fairweather or Sears unsettled me. Sheen of black fabric, shoulders not quite padded but squared, pant hems I'd have to take down; I looked like I'd read *The 7 Habits of Highly Effective People* without enough conviction. A suit, like any aspirational purchase, leads to further acquisitions; it doesn't pair well with salt-ravaged boots or a duffel coat mended with bright yarn. I'd never felt so unlike myself in any other garment, not even the bulky, elastic-waisted, sea-green trousers my grandmother sewed for me when I was nine.

Unmooring a boat won't cause much drift at first—a subtle turn, a soft knock against the wharf. My parents rarely entered spaces where people wore formal clothing, and my friends considered suits to be symbolic of capitalism. For a few hours, I wore the estranging outfit, and it worked: in the waiting room on interview day, I resembled the other candidates, which meant I hadn't disqualified myself before I spoke. And when I did, was my voice in costume as well? Monochrome, ironed, hung.

Two school buses take us to the barbeque. A few students already know the Dean; he's a great guy, they say. A regressive, quaking ride: no seatbelts, knees wedged. Farms and woodlots scroll past the yellowed windows. We reach a house with terraced gardens and a turquoise pool; the water glitters undisturbed. The Dean is tall and wears a polo shirt. Influence exudes from where he stands, holding a drink, solar centre to a planetary audience that laughs deferentially, makes pitches of their own ambitions.

Small clusters of others hover around the pool with paper plates of food. Past the flower beds and chain-link fence, patches of burdock, thistles, vetches, and milkweed stir inside the cricket hum. I've met people who would recognize that dry ground as apothecary; for us it forms a backdrop to strategic conversations.

The clean sound of a splash. A student has started to swim laps in a fast and deliberate backstroke, his goggled face focused, pale torso gliding under a thin film of water. He swims for a long time, back and forth as if scanning across a dial and not finding the right station.

I meet the Dean only once, almost three and a half years later. Now I have worn a range of disguises—pleated blouse, pencil skirt, white coat, surgical scrubs, lead apron—and understand their limits in transforming the one who wears them. Even if I loop a paper mask around my ears. Even if I'm able to make a case presentation without rehearsal, am willing to concede that some knowledge is found through randomized controlled clinical trials, and is not like Elizabeth Bishop's: *dark, salt, clear, moving, utterly free, / drawn from the cold hard mouth / of the world.*

The Dean works in an office of dark wood, inside a historic white building, near where Lake Ontario's breakers wash the limestone slabs. Like every student, I spend a few minutes with him to review what he will write in his letter for my residency application. I've added everything to my CV that seems potentially relevant, and in the publications section are a number of literary works and prizes. He frowns at the page, holding an expensive pen, then peers over his glasses at me and asks, Are these scientific articles? When I shake my head, he slashes a line through the list.

///

Our main lecture hall is underground. Swivel chairs softly press our rib cages against the desks. The anatomy course, one semester long, follows a rigorous tempo; we label diagrams almost frantically, our hands cramping. The thorax is first. Learning to call the armpit the axilla, naming its five walls of muscle. Distinguishing the shapes of the right and left lungs. Finding the junction where the lymph enters the blood. I love this merger of architecture and language. Coracoid, resembling a raven. Supraclavicular, over the bone that moves like a key.

The theory is graceful line drawings, words in scrawled shorthand; the practise awaits in metal caskets. My group is assigned to body number eight, an elderly female. Ashen nipples flattened by the metal lid, toenails longer than seems decent. Her head is a featureless white oval. All the heads have been wrapped in gauze; they are like Magritte's renditions of *The Lovers*, but here the figures are nude and supine, evenly spaced throughout the large room. Graduate students do the dissections, so we only have to look and point and touch and name. The bodies do not resemble the illustrations in the atlas. Major arteries and veins have been injected with dyes, but the flesh is otherwise dull and confluent, like raw chicken. An art class memory flashes through me: I carved a beet into an anatomical heart shape, placed it in an old clarinet case lined with blue velour. The sweet, sharp, earthen smell, magenta stains remaining on my palms. We're breakable, our hearts should make music. We're breakable, somebody has to repair us.

Remembering not to scratch my face or adjust my ponytail or reach into my pockets. The lab director doesn't tolerate wallflowers. Get in there, he urges, touch every organ. I lift the heavy, sodden liver, feel the frigid fluid trickle down my wrist. Confirm the rigidity of the windpipe. I'm inclined to handle the cadaver as if it still holds a sensing, volitional presence, but otherwise relieved to find myself capable of what's required. After a while, the smell stops turning my stomach, even when we go from the lab straight to the pub for wings. This dismantling of the body is a rite of passage, and earlier students were willing to sneak into cemeteries with shovels for the experience. Now I learn the finer rites within this one, in unexpected locales like the forearm; pulling at a tendon in that dense and complicated bundle of muscles, predicting which joint in which finger will move. Memorizing the cranial nerves and the openings through which they leave the skull. Their subsequent branches. At home I draw a poster of the brain as a jellyfish, trailing tendrils.

On certain evenings, the anatomy museum is open for study. A lighter atmosphere, students patiently instructing each other. Some know the muscles well from working out. The pleasure of being in a room with such a surplus of intelligence; even the casual conversations are complex, funny, intriguing. Our blurred reflections move across a gleaming cooler full of human limbs.

I was seven or eight years old when I first said I wanted to be a doctor, and I witnessed the effect on my father: an animation in his voice, the glaze gone from his eyes. That foreign light of his benign attention. I wanted other things over the years, but couldn't resist the submerged, magnetic idea that me becoming a doctor would transform him. Now I subdue a lurking disquiet. As I examine the vasculature of a plastinated stomach, someone taps me on the shoulder. It's the mock history student, but he's using the hand of a severed arm.

Every week, the cadavers have been altered to reveal another layer of organ systems or muscle groups.

Their odour worsens, they slacken and unravel, will not be reassembled into sleeping humans. A question arises about the face. It is imminent in our lectures. The atlas shows the bands of muscle across the cheeks, the secret, hollow antlers of the sinuses. Will they remove the gauze? There are students who say yes, and others who claim that the decay has already gone too far. On lab day, I feel uneasy; I've left finger dents inside this woman's lungs, and now I may have to truly encounter her.

The bandages are gone. Reading a face, an elemental form of literacy. This one has a childlike nose and narrow lips, the air of being unamused by nonsense, of harbouring an unmentioned hurt—but the expression is also a trick, made unreliable because it has been quartered with a saw. The preceptor pulls at the cheeks, and the face falls open. It is shaped like that folded paper craft of grade school recesses, worn on the thumbs and fingers—pick a number, here's your fortune. Show me the child at seven: I read, I drew, I found it hard to look at the dried mealworms that my friend fed to his turtle. Three hours after the lab doors open, when I hang my white coat on a locker's hook, I know what rites are for; that I am subtly different now from who I was in the morning, from everyone who hasn't encountered such a thing. That there is no return from this departure.

///

My computer's monitor occupies much of a card table, and the hard drive breathes like a French bulldog on the worn carpet below. I'm reading an online article one night when the screen's image abruptly shrinks to a green spot and is gone. Dark reflection. This malfunction is the possible loss of all my study notes: I write them in class, then type them at home, add details from the textbooks; for exams, I print out and study my compilations, draw diagrams. The files span hundreds of evenings of work, but they are not what registers as loss. Outside, the streetlamp's downcast eye begins to flicker in a citric yellow that steadies, then slowly warms to the richness of butter, a sight that usually pleases me. Now there is only a galloping, escaped feeling, a form of panic. The computer holds two documents that are the openings of short stories; I started writing them while reading Grace Paley, and then wishing to be as good as her stalled me. In the first, a student stands at the window on the twelfth floor of a campus building, watching streams of other students walking to their classes. In the second, a girl is repeatedly mistaken for another who is missing from her neighbourhood. This drowning dread I feel, there is no sense in it; the stories are fragmentary, vestigial, less narratives than premises. I want them like I want my life.

I call my friend at the other end of the country. I'm worried for you, says her gentle voice. She is pursuing a degree in creative writing—a waste, my father has told me. When I differ with him, I have to tighten my gut, steady my voice against an annihilation. I'm five years out from the house that remains furnished with his views, an interior I once knew as the only house, as life's hollow axle. The reading lamp casts my enormous shadow. I press the worn wire into the phone while I hold the receiver, otherwise the connection breaks. I know what I'm doing, I answer.

I'm imagining versions of being a doctor that would feel right. With a pilot's license or a bicycle. With straightforward interventions like drugs against malaria or HIV. Makeshift strategies for overcoming a lack of supplies. In communities that are stubborn and resilient, where improvisation and making things of beauty remain essential practices. When I picture that place, I believe I know what I'm doing.

I start clerkship at a family medicine clinic in a red brick house with a turret. After two and a half years of lectures, the work feels wondrous and exhausting. Lists of names that materialize as real people. Casting questions into the waters of their reticence, or volubility, or trouble remembering, or certainty of what is wrong. One of the doctors makes house calls. In a high-rise apartment, we visit an elderly woman with big artificial eyelashes who wears an asbestos apron as protection from her own discarded cigarettes. We have to turn down the opera to speak with her. Another patient is asleep with his cat in the loft of his house, each room as cluttered with antiques as a flea market. I start to know the city differently: streets and brick and limestone houses are the visible architecture, but the true substance is a constantly elapsing stream of narratives, with all the rhythms and junctions of a living system.

Every day, I struggle to discipline my attention. I shouldn't long to distil the nature of a city or wonder over the sense of self that would affix the eyelashes but not bother with an ashtray. There is too much else to know. In the clinic, the shape of my listening alters, loses its trawler-net feeling. My mind starts to work in schematics. As I focus on medical histories and physical examinations, my vision of the people themselves seems less clear.

The writing I do now is in charts, at the clinic and then on the wards. Concise, uninflected, painstakingly accurate. The blue binders are objects of strange powers. What they hold will often supersede the patient's claims. The past and the future are there: records of what has happened, orders for what's to be done. Medical language pretends there is no writer, but even the range of handwriting says otherwise: narrow, scrawled, slanted, cryptic, squared. My hand still knows the feeling of my own first writing, formed along lines that were floors and ceilings for the short and tall parts of the letters. Then the plump, upright printing—i's dotted with circles or suns or hearts—that denoted being a girl. Later, tight lecture notes that merged printing and cursive; this is the script I use in the charts, condensing words and phrases into acronyms as if closing umbrellas. I'm writing for two readers, neither of whom are the subject: the next health care worker and the hypothetical lawyer. A version of Leonard Cohen's lines about a kite flow through my mind—*a chart is a victim you are sure of / you love it because it pulls / gentle enough to call you master / strong enough to call you fool.*

The conventions of writing in a hospital chart are straightforward. A limited vocabulary is applied in a predictable sequence to describe the protagonist's medical condition. Across the terse facts, a narrative arc forms of its own accord and ends with one of three resolutions: discharge, transfer, or death. A short story, on the other hand, has no scaffolding rules. That freefall through all possibilities—I hear it in the stories of the patients: in the manner of its telling, no life is like another. The digressions that hinder a consultation's progress are the territory of that distinctiveness. When possible, I listen for what makes the patient sound stirred, feeling, present, and then ask them about that. I don't write from those narrative scraps: they feel too privately given. The material I have claim to is my own.

Earlier in medical school, a poem of mine is published by a magazine based in a bigger city. It arrives in the mail; they've placed the text over an image of a woman with a stroller in a grocery store. Whenever I open that page, I glance at her face, which looks young and maternally tired, framed by straight dark hair tied back. And then one afternoon in the pediatric clinic, I enter the consultation room to find a mother with a boy. The restless flicker of a recognition I can't name. I ask the proper questions, but am also working something out—and then I have it: she is the woman under the poem. Oh, right, she says, I know the editor, they asked for that picture, we've moved since then. She isn't all that interested because her child is sick. *Write,* Grace Paley said, *what will stop your breath if you don't write.*

///

I'm assigned to obstetrics in another, smaller city. Their hospital has terrazzo hallways, narrow elevators that stop and start as if they're hand-cranked from the basement. A boxed sign, X-Ray In Use. A security office with a sliding window so high that I never see who works there; I hand up the form to get my ID, and the voice says they like my ring. Every once in a while, the building shudders due to detonations in the bedrock of the grounds where the new hospital will be. I watch the tremors on the surface of my coffee.

The rotation consists of eight shifts that are twenty-four hours long, with the same interval of rest between them. The labour and delivery ward has a storage room with a cot, but the quiet hours are short, and when I lie down beside the shelves of institutional cleaning products, my sleep feels like a smudged photocopy of the real thing. After two or three rounds, I forget to be hungry. At eight in the morning I'm either walking back to my apartment, tired but too vivid with impressions to sleep, or returning to the hospital, determined to summon alertness in spite of an insistent undertow. Colours seem starker. The traffic sounds weakly out of tune.

The work itself turns the world more translucent still: witnessing the arrival of newly formed humans, blue-tinged and wailing, duplicate and unrepeatable. One newborn emerges without making a sound, storm-blue eyes wide open and gazing attentively into mine. Anne Stevenson: *The spirit is too blunt an instrument / to have made this baby.*

One night, a doctor suddenly orders me to participate. Fright, exhilaration. The room, humid with sweat and amniotic fluid, has resounded with effort, encouragement, pain. Now the parents, watching the infant between the mother's legs, have taken on the proportions of gods. Their baby cries hoarsely. I am full of a current of feeling that is vast and dark and scattered with stars. It seems to root me to the floor.

Cut the cord, the attending says.

I turn slowly to the equipment cart. Metal instruments gleam on blue paper. Willing my gloved hand to move, I pick up a hemostat. A nurse, drying the baby with a towel, makes room for me. The cord feels thick and slippery and alive. I clamp down the tool and lift the scissors. Cut the cord! the doctor repeats. I'm holding the rubbery, damp tube between my fingers; it is pulsing. Wait until the pulsing stops, says the vast feeling. It is not so much compelling as entirely pervasive.

Cut it! the doctor snaps. I want to articulate what I perceive, but then he's shouting, and the mother looks at us, and the nurse nudges my shoulder, and I press the scissors through the beating cord. Blood spurts out; fine droplets spray onto the wall, the side of the father's head, the telephone by the bedside. I've missed that what's required is two hemostats, and then a cut between them. Thank goodness for nurses. They wipe the father's temple; he is so awed by his baby that he seems almost unaware. They take the scissors from me gently. The doctor swears and walks out.

I'm speechless. I want to claim that I'm good with my hands, that I've drawn blood gases in the middle of the night, and started an IV on someone thrashing in their bed; the urge to declare my competence blazes almost uncontainably, but how will anything I say speak louder than what I've done?

One day, years afterwards, I will attend a lecture on Indigenous medicines. An Oneida medicine man will say that it is customary, in his culture, to wait for the umbilical pulse to fade out before cutting the cord. He says it means the spirit has arrived. A long exhalation: this practice exists, it doesn't endanger the child. He tells us that in his tradition it takes twenty years of apprenticeship to become a healer.

For now, I am lying on a cot in the call room that's a storage closet, waiting for the burn of my mistake to turn to embers. And it does, during the days that follow, as I clamp cords twice and cut them cleanly, learn to feel for cervical dilation, use the Doppler on the fetal heart, watch the first breath enter furrowed little faces, and suppress the vast feeling when it comes, although somewhere I still register the disturbance.

///

After almost three months of continuous Internal Medicine rotations, the hospital saturates my consciousness. When I pass through the park, it seems cinematically beautiful in contrast—a green sea flecked with purple clover, leaf shadows flickering on the grass, children tumbling and sprinting across the playground. Under the broad maples, lapsed versions of me are lying on a blanket, reading, pausing to stare at the sky while the words sink inward.

Until I was there too often, the hospital was compelling as an idea, an isthmus in the trajectory of thousands of lives. People came in to work their shifts. To hear what was wrong. To wait out dialysis. Lie still in a scanner. Be opened and altered and stitched shut. Convalesce. Give birth. Leave this world. It seemed novelistically layered and grand.

The outer door feels too heavy. That sensation from dreams, of moving against a pervasive resistance. Once inside, I feel less literate. I misread the hierarchies among people in scrubs; I can't find the conference rooms. At first, I wanted to overhaul the design. What if every bed faced a window, and mobiles of birds floated overhead, and ocean-coloured mosaics covered the walls? Surely the meals didn't have to arrive industrially frozen in transport trucks. I found journal articles on the elaborate and efficient kitchens of Chinese hospitals and showed them to my attendings. I brought patients books from the library they might like. But soon my senses started protesting, and now my disillusionment has grown visceral, unreasoned, infinite. I want to escape the tedium of morning rounds, and I'm sick of the glue-textured muffins that await in the call wing, of tearing their wrapping with hands raw from washing, and I don't want to enter another morosely toned ward room that smells of bagged urine, pulling the curtain aside to ask a stranger intrusive questions. Everyone, myself included, seems like a cog in the building's bleak machine.

I imagine my objections as principled, rooted in ethics and aesthetics, and then I doubt myself—because the hospital is a collective ruse, a place of faith in the reductive and separate, and I am surrounded by believers. My classmates sound eager to be in the building, mastering its workings, close to doing what doctors do. I begin to wonder if my aversion has other roots. My father dreads hospitals—you go in, you don't come out, is what his own father told him of the Nairobi institutions. But doctors, when I hear those generations speak of them, still seem adjacent to gods.

I am not becoming a god. I'm studying real people who are ill, and it is troubling to find my own dejection outweighing my consideration for their suffering. If compassion is the godlike thing inside of me, medical training is making it shrink. In my journal, I quote Sylvia Plath: *each night, now, I must capture one taste, one touch, one vision from the ruck of the day's garbage.* Then I stop writing at all. My boyfriend gives me *The Birth of the Clinic* as consolation, and reading it makes me lonelier.

When I get out on time, I go to kickboxing class. A warehouse space with plywood walls, fluorescent lights in their last spasms, the funk of sweat gone old. We do sit-ups while a partner slams a pad into our abdomen. Practise roundhouse kicks originally meant to strike and rupture the opponent's kidney. Slam our shins against foam-covered posts to harden the bone. It feels right to me, like a dance, a performance of the grim and sleepless rotations: doing a steeling thing with gritted teeth.

There's only one difference, the instructor says, in training women, and it's getting them past their unwillingness to hit someone with full force. With me, he's right. It takes months before I am willing to attempt it on a volunteer, his friendly smile inside the helmet's frame. I punch, still holding back, and then he goads me until the brakes lift, and I truly hit him, and his head reels back. I feel a clamour of elation, regret, power, concern. What has shattered momentarily—the idea of not doing harm? In the morning, I'll return to ward rounds at the hospital, and the doctor and residents will speak with the patients. We'll dispense a measured, distracted kindness, not the whole force we are capable of inhabiting.

Now, Dr. G. says, you're going to accompany them—follow what happens from this moment of admission, because once you're a physician, you'll no longer have that chance. He is a white-haired respirologist with wild eyebrows and thin, burst veins on his cheeks. At our first meeting, he asked which remaining group of workers can still smoke as much they want, and I stared at the floor for what felt like ages and then said truck drivers, which made him grin. I've heard that Dr. G. smokes cigarettes himself.

He means I should accompany the couple in the clinic room. They are seated in plastic chairs. The patient is thin, wearing a Black Sabbath T-shirt, and has a greying mustache. His girlfriend's knees are shaking. For half a year, the man's shoulder has ached, a problem first attributed to lifting pallets at his workplace. He was prescribed ibuprofen and physiotherapy. When the pain worsened, the family doctor ordered a chest X-ray. I have seen it. The white spun sugar mass in the apex of his right lung. His lung, but not his mass: the tumour is the foreign body that the known body has made.

Dr. G. has told the patient it is stage IV cancer, and inoperable, and that he will be admitted immediately for radiation and chemotherapy. I've watched the man absorb this news with breathtaking equanimity. He may, like in the Raymond Carver poem, have thanked the doctor. I'm holding the chart with the admission note that Dr. G. has helped me write, and I lead the patient and his girlfriend down the hallway that goes from the clinic wing into the wards, aware that I barely know what to do. This must be overwhelming, I hear my voice say, but things are moving in the right direction now; you're starting treatment. The couple nods and follows, holding hands.

We get to the nursing station, and I introduce myself to the person I think is the ward clerk but could also be the charge nurse, or another nurse sitting down to use the computer. I'm ignored. During clerkship, it seems possible to be simultaneously invisible and in the way. Undercurrents of race and gender; almost all the nurses and administrators at this hospital are white women, but a good number of my classmates are from South or East Asian immigrant families. The grace of having a mistake attributed to inexperience is not for us. But another nurse repeats my introduction to the first, and then the system begins to work. The patient fills out registration forms, receives a wristband from one place, a gown from another. His girlfriend leaves to collect an overnight bag for him. A bed is assigned, his vital signs are monitored, he selects a meal plan with the dietary aide. The oncologist explains the chemotherapy: durations, statistics, side effects. More blood is drawn. The girlfriend returns, a brother arrives. Long intervals of waiting. I stay, not doing much, answering and asking a few questions, making sure the patient doesn't have to repeat himself too often when new staff come in. I read my respirology notes. Dr. G. stops by, says the radiation oncology team is behind schedule, so their resident will come after hours instead. The sinking feeling of an extended sentence: I'm not on call, but now I will be there late.

I visit the cafeteria before it closes, pushing my tray along the ledge, taking an orange pekoe bag, lifting the lever for water that's never quite hot enough for tea. I order the crab cakes, and the doctor in line beside me jokes that I'll need my stomach pumped, but nothing is funny, I'm too involuted in my own gloom. I eat quickly, skimming a newspaper, hoping not to miss the radiation oncologist. Returning upstairs, I observe the consult, translate it afterwards for the brother. Then we're done.

I know, when I gather my things from the windowsill to leave, that there's a summer night outside the window, but the glass holds only the contours of the room. We're alone for a moment, this stranger and I, his family out for a break, and then a young woman who looks like him comes in. When I turn, she is hugging the patient in his bed, her face wet with tears. It's too intimate, too close to what I wish my own life held; I look away. When the patient introduces his daughter, he says of me, very deliberately, I think she's going to be a really good doctor.

///

Several of the doctors I study with are deeply, memorably good at their work. Any practice can be an art—the line cook who makes a choreography of cracking eggs and flipping pancakes, the kindergarten teacher who slowly draws the shy child out of hiding and there are family doctors like that, and surgeons, and nephrologists. But Dr. R. is exceptional.

I find him without looking. In the hallway outside the undergraduate office, I see a hurriedly made poster for an elective in a small, distant city, meant to draw future physicians: They cover the flight and room and board, and all specialties are available. No further debt. I email them, requesting hematology. I like the dimensions of what happens in the blood. Legible clues: red blood cells that are too small or large, or the wrong shape, or too few in number. The immune system's endless riddles. The serial reaction that makes a clot, one part of which was elucidated by Leo Vroman, who is also one of my favourite poets. *A human is a soft machine / a bendable column with holes / stuffed full of slender wires / and little tubes that serve / nothing but tenderness,* he wrote. Practically, this elective will complement another one in HIV/AIDS medicine. As the plane descends, I take in the sight of a river without water, its bed the colour of rust.

I'm in Dr. R.'s clinic before he arrives, a good start. Less promising is that he's a general oncologist; his hematology practice is confined to Thursday evenings. The cancer centre at my regular hospital occupies an entire building, with specialists in every type of tumour, but here Dr. R. has two consultation rooms and one recently hired colleague. He walks in slowly, a round man wearing owlish glasses, sits down at a desk too small for him, and starts signing forms. He mutters to the paperwork for a while, scolds his computer, asks some questions of the nurses. Then he gets up laboriously, reads my nametag out loud, and shrugs, Okay, let's go see the first patient.

A medical history consists of the doctor interviewing the patient on their condition. The one at a first appointment should be comprehensive; later, specific and shorter. For students, the list of questions is a script, and the concern is forgetting a line. The asking can sound mechanical. Now I watch Dr. R. elicit all the necessary information in what seems like a natural exchange. He's warm and humorous and honest. Hears patients out when they mention their vacations, or grandchildren, or nightmares. An elderly woman cries over the worry of recurrence, and he puts a hand on her shoulder and says, Make like a duck, have you seen the ducks, the water flows right off the feathers. She hugs him.

For the physical exams, Dr. R. does only what's essential, his practice distilled by experience—though some elements seem closer to a form of magic. I watch him brush his hand briefly across someone's abdomen and then tell me the dimensions of their liver for the chart. I confirm it later through the patient's CT: he is exactly right. He must also feel the tumour's growth, occasionally, or hear the new onset of heart failure through his stethoscope, but he never reveals alarm.

My existence that May is monastically self-contained. I stay in a suburban house a few doors down from the hospital with three physiotherapy students and a surgery resident who makes sporadic appearances. My room is in the basement, with a small window below the street, shag carpet, a contingent of thick spiders. There's a common landline and no internet. I've been given hospital meal vouchers, useful for lunches but not breakfasts or dinners due the clinic and ward hours. Late into the evenings, Dr. R. sits at his desk and dictates correspondence into a machine that occasionally transcribes his exhalations as the word *where*. His secretary deletes these insertions in the morning. I hear him petition pharmaceutical companies on behalf of individual patients who cannot afford their treatments; he starts those letters with *Dear People*.

Essentially, I am asleep at the house and awake at the hospital. On the weekends, I do groceries, sit on the back step barefoot, watch robins arrive on the lawn. I drink sweet, strong coffee and send tourist postcards to friends. I call my parents. In April, I stayed with them during my elective at the HIV/AIDS clinic. I would soon be a doctor, and it didn't matter; my father remained as he was. We were sitting in the backyard on the first warm day when he said he could no longer smile, then showed me the grimace of trying. I told him carefully it sounded like depression, but the conversation sputtered out. At the student house, the phone is in the hallway and the others can hear me. Afterwards, I'm clumsier, I want to be alone.

The neighbourhood is edged by wooded hills that look made for roaming, so I hike a road to its end, where a resident warns me of mountain lions. One weekend, I get on a bus to the nearest larger city, like a sailor taking leave. Otherwise, I'm immersed in the rotation. Dr. R. doesn't tell me to study, but I read everything because he makes the work intriguing. The types of solid tumours, the malignancies of the blood. Practising bone marrow biopsies. Asking not whether a patient has noticed a change in their hearing, but whether they've been turning up the radio.

I try to parse what makes Dr. R. virtuosic. His knowledge is almost flawless. His diagnostic skills seem supernatural. At instances when it should be impossible, he makes patients laugh. His presence steadies them. My empathy is less mature, and every so often, I feel the urge to protest fate: not this docile father of young children, not this high school athlete, not this bent woman with no one to look after her. Dr. R. is moved by his patients—a nurse tells me that he bought a bicycle for a child whose mother died, and once I watch him stare for a silent minute at a scan that indicates recurrence—but he exudes the feeling that nothing disturbs him. His gaze seems older than the world.

We attend an expensive dinner funded by a pharmaceutical company, followed by a presentation promoting their latest drug, and he leans over to me and whispers, You know, once in a while it's okay to relax your principles and enjoy a really good lobster.

One evening, as I stifle a yawn, he says over his shoulder, Go home early, you've worked hard. And at the end of the month, he says, You'd be wasted on family medicine. An archaic compliment, meant well—but I hear the closing of the James Wright poem whose speaker is lying in a hammock, and concludes without regret, *I have wasted my life*.

Dr. R. doesn't know that I doubt practising medicine altogether, and I can't imagine telling him—he is too brilliant a physician, and I am too far along in my training. The rotation has been almost inversely instructive. I've seen the sacrifices of giving yourself to your patients—that your mind will be a medical archive, that your own health might be compromised, that your spouse will have to attend to almost everything else for you—but it's not the potential deterrents that stay with me: observing doctoring as a calling, I'm persuaded that it should only be done in that spirit.

///

Medical school is four years of impressions in dense accumulation—coded, privileged, unnerving, almost impossible to consolidate. There are days when I feel purposeful. Rotating through an addictions clinic, I bike home and am gratified to hear Goodnight doc! shouted from a cluster of unhoused people in the nearby park. I immerse myself in books on the philosophy of psychiatry, interview HIV/AIDS patients about their metaphors for the immune system, present research on gender discrimination in the hidden curriculum. During a surgery elective, I observe the correction of a neonatal cardiac condition that is otherwise fatal within the first year of life: a miracle of human accomplishment, the baby on the vast table, a churning machine standing in for the heart and lungs, surgeons stitching tiny vessels into place. And still, and still, and still—I envy with a sickening ache any friend or acquaintance who works at painting or writing or dancing.

One afternoon, my pager goes off as I wait in the surgery lounge. I call the number: it's my friend who hasn't really studied 1826. Come out to the hall, he says. He holds the door to the stairwell open—stairs we've taken at all hours, hurrying to rounds, trailing verbose attendings, answering calls, stethoscopes looped in our pockets—and I hear a cavernous gushing. Water from some upper rupture pours in clear sheets down the risers, scallops over the landings, bundles its transparent muscles turning corners in the downward spiral of the stairs. When a ritual works, you possess a new knowledge. *If you tasted it, it would first taste bitter, then briny, then surely burn your tongue.*

Not long after starting, I leave my residency program. I don't feel free, but at fault. There is a shortage of family doctors, and my supervisor tries to reason with me—everyone I speak with does. I don't know how to tell my parents. They were frugal so that I could study what I did; frugal enough that I can still afford to stop. My father calls me things it takes a lifetime to forget. My mother says it's hardest on her. At my own kitchen table, during those clouded months of living in the city while no longer having a reason to be there or a means to afford the rent, I start writing again.

The apartment faces a small Russian Orthodox church, and in my story, the narrator's does as well. She is studying fine arts but has told her family her program is architecture. From her window, she sees some people cross themselves when they pass the red brick church, an automated, offhand gesture: a boy on a skateboard, dragging his sneaker along the ground to slow down; a woman in a car, adjusting her rear-view mirror in the same motion. The priest lives in an adjacent apartment. He sits in a lawn chair, making calls, drinking V8. He returns greetings with a small nod, eyes closed, as if he parcels out his attention so frequently that he struggles to conserve some for himself.

This story is one that I finish, and then it goes through rounds of submission and rejection and revision. One rejection comes with an encouraging note written in the margin of the form letter. We liked, they say, how it ends.

I pass over a stone threshold, smooth and sunken with use. There is an entranceway with pamphlets filed into slots in the wall. All of them are in Russian except one that says 'Information about the Orthodox Church,' and I take it. Then I move into the body of the church. There are no pews. Beams of soft, dust-filled light fall through the stained-glass windows, landing on the bare floor in flecks of colour. At the far end, carpeted steps lead to an altar covered in candles, and the wall behind it is crammed with images of angels and saints. Every surface and curve is painted gold or vermilion or blue. The air smells of incense and old wood.

A mechanical roar is coming from a hallway. The priest is there, off to the side and facing a large, portable fan with his arms out, his purple robe fluttering in the current of air. When he sees me, he bends down wearily to turn off the machine, pushing at stuck buttons before pulling the plug from the wall. In the sudden silence that follows, he asks, "What you take?" and I hold up the pamphlet for him to see. He nods his solemn approval and says, "You are going now, goodbye."

And then, when I've already turned to go, "Bless you."

IN THE FIELD

I played frog calls on the car's tape deck. The windows had to be closed to hear them, and because it was summer in Southwestern Ontario, and the car was old, the heat and humidity were almost trance-inducing. After two turns, the drive followed a single road, from the neighbourhood of Victorian mansions and sentinel maples where I rented a house with other students, past the downtown's chemically weedless park, City Hall, and office towers with glass walls that showed the clouds, through an urban residential stretch of worn houses and pawn shops with iron grates, across a wide intersection where hospitals the size of factories loomed, along parking lots, a mall, the Value Village, fast food signs that registered even when I wasn't really looking, over the big highway, and by one last building, a Catholic high school, before the city gave way to yellow fields. The tape's speaker repeated *Ra-na cla-mi-tans*, in a bored, unwilling tone. The green frog's voice, which I heard constantly at the ponds, was a plucked string without a soundbox.

I was working for a professor named Kee. He knew the geology of the city, where there were moraines and buried creeks. He told me that trees hold so many symbiotic bacteria that if their wood and leaves were somehow erased, they would still look like phantoms of themselves. Kee had given me the frog tape and loaned me his car, which had tiny animal bones on the dashboard, and water-stained field guides and philosophy books all over the seats. He and his wife Patricia's project at Kirk-Cousins, a small conservation area which they renamed with what Kee called an Iroquois word—A'Nowaghi, place of the turtles—was to attempt an inventory of every species present within its bounds. They hoped this list would inspire the public towards conservationism. An odd crew of hired experts and improvisers, including botanists, birders, herpetologists, and biology students like myself, were to spend the summer on this study.

My job was to identify the resident aquatic insects. I worked alone. I started out with a *Peterson Field Guide*, a dip net, a jar, and waders.

From the parking lot, the ponds that I was assigned to survey were reachable by two routes. One ran diagonally across a meadow and then rambled through the woods. Some mornings that meadow stalled me: I would use the dipnet to catch and release leopard frogs or admire the wildflowers or wander to the corner where the mantises with their green skull faces rested on blades of grass. The forested part of the trail sloped down and then up. In the valley was a den, and sometimes the red fox who lived there skimmed through the ferns to disappear underground. The place seemed small and contained enough to imagine that it held one of everything: one fox, one ancient snapping turtle, one great oak.

The alternate way in was to follow a railway track straight from a corner of the parking lot: a short, broiling route, the footing made awkward by steep gravel edges. The rails were in use, and once in a long while an engine with four or five cargo cars would clatter north or south. But the wooded trail had a boggy section clouded with mosquitoes, so I usually took the tracks. At first, I glanced over my shoulder constantly, then I was able to do this less by keeping my ear attuned to a rumble, and eventually I learned to feel for the train's distant approach through my sneakers on the metal line.

To draw up the net and examine what it held was a gesture that hovered between work and a return to the fertile mud of childhood. The fresh burst of water draining, the green tinsel of weeds. I got to know the ponds' common characters: striders, boatmen with their wide oar legs, backswimmers who held their silvery air supply on their bellies, and the small scarlet dots that were water mites. Whirligigs took repeated efforts to catch. And once, when I dragged the net low, it surfaced with a slender, stick-like insect about two inches long—the elusive water scorpion! My arm was so far out that my balance wavered, and the creature immediately darted over the net's edge and dove. I kept the insects I collected in a jar and dried them out at home—a passive killing that required no overt cruelty from me. At the end of the week, I would drive to the campus and, in the dust of an empty lab, use a microscope and reference books to make identifications, which could hinge on details like the number of barbs on a rear leg. There was a day when I left the ponds early because the catch was so good: an enormous brown bug, two diving beetles, a water spider, and what I thought might be a pygmy backswimmer. I put the jar, with its soft algal glow, in the passenger seat. At a red light close to home, I picked it up to admire the collection. There was only one living insect: the giant water bug. A voracious predator, I later read. It had drained all the others to scraps and husks.

The ponds made me think of Kafka's remark: *Do not even listen, simply wait, be quiet, still and solitary. The world will freely offer itself to you to be unmasked, it has no choice, it will roll in ecstasy at your feet.* I could wade into the shallows or push out in the canoe stored on the bank—its sides would get studded with leaches—and actively fish for insects, but it was when I did nothing that the life of the pond adjusted to my presence: then the trees were rooted to their own inverted doubles in the water's mirror, turtles surfaced like small islands, less common frogs began to call out, and a regal blue heron circled down to land in the reeds, while along the shore two weasels gave each other mercurial chase. The pattern of light refracted through the wings of a turquoise dragonfly at rest on the end of a reed, in its irregular alternations between bright angular stars and a diffuse oval glow, might become interpretable. Although I had my particular assignment, all life forms were to be noted down. The process felt different then: receptive, immersive, full of good luck.

On a day in July, a small team of people—Kee, a Ministry of Natural Resources representative, a fish biologist, another student, and myself—went to assess the fish life in another pond. The MNR worker carried a large, heavy battery from his van. He was soon red and struggling to breathe, and I was concerned for him. Other than Kee, the men I worked with that summer, including the entomologist who verified my identifications, often seemed to acknowledge or address only each other; the ministry worker waved away my offer of help. He left very deep prints in the mud. At the shore, the fish expert put on waders and went in. The battery sent its shock through the water and instantly dozens of fish were on their sides at the surface, their stunned eyes on the sky. The biologist, turning in a circle, muttered names and numbers into a voice recorder. The voltage had been calibrated to immobilize most fish for ten seconds—after that, only ripples remained.

There were moments when I felt a sense of risk while at the ponds. When the only other car in the parking lot belonged to a man who said, as I took gear from the trunk, that I had great form. On the tracks, after a hiker mentioned that once every summer a rail vehicle with two spinning blades would come to strip the brush where I sheltered when the train passed, and its driver might not see me. And for a time in August, after Kee called my house to say that a tiger was missing from an exotic animal farm somewhere near A'Nowaghi, but that it was older and had been declawed and would not be a danger. He sounded too disinterested, even in confirming he was serious, to be joking. There was no reliable local news on the internet then; I couldn't find a listed private zoo either.

For a few days, every rustle of the grasses, every snapped twig at my back, would detonate in my chest as I scanned the undergrowth for a striped flank, a whiskered head. Was there, among the dwellers of these woods, one tiger? There was one of me. At the end of the week, I saw Kee at the lab. It came back home, he shrugged, it was probably hungry.

Some experiences make such clear or commonplace sense that they do not persist inside of us. Working at the ponds was not like that—my mind turns that work over and over, as the raccoon who was once at the water did with a shell. Kee and Patricia's study went on for three years and expanded to include geology, hydrology, and history. The resulting bio-survey listed 1,028 species: among them were the paramecium, the sweetbread mushroom, the elm bark moss, the sensitive fern, the leafy satin grass, the eastern swallowtail, the deerfly, the green heron, the slippery elm, the shagbark hickory, the red fox, the sugar maple, and the white-footed mouse. I've considered the gap between naming creatures and knowing them. The nature of lists: That they fail to describe relationships, except perhaps in the ranking implied by their order. That taking inventory is first of all a component of trade. I've questioned killing or shocking other life forms as a form of study, allegedly for their own ultimate good. I've marvelled at how a possible tiger immediately integrated me as an animal part of the environment. I've thought about the working group that included me only at its margins. That the Linnaean taxonomy system we relied on had once classified humans by race. That our methods to know the land gave primacy to the visual, even though that turned out to be an impractical way for me to keep assessing if a train was coming. And I've been aware that an Indigenous presence was alluded to only in a borrowed name in Iroquoian, a European term that may have derogatory origins, and designates an entire group of languages: Tuscarora, whose last fluent speaker died in 2019, but passed on much of his knowledge in teachings and recordings; Oneida; Onondaga; Cayuga; Seneca; and Kanien'kéha, which has thousands of fluent speakers and two immersion schools.

When I was sitting on a boulder and watching the pond's world roll at my feet, still forming only a limited awareness of what it possessed in shapes, contingencies, bonds, conversations, spirits, threats, resemblances, seductions, and nourishments, I could feel myself pressing against a cloud of ignorance: not only a lack of knowledge but a lack of the means to know. In the decades since then, I have been fortunate to start perceiving nature differently, through listening to local Indigenous people's conceptions of land and plants and animals, and spending more time in the woods simply waiting. That fog of not knowing has shrunk around its edges, but the bulk of it remains, because it isn't possible or ethical for me to make Indigenous cultural and linguistic perspectives my own.

The monarch butterfly, also on the biosurvey list, has been recently declared endangered. Two new gravel quarries, each as large as the conservation site itself, now operate nearby. The weather of the region has grown volatile and strange. If I could return to that earlier work at the ponds, which I often loved, I wouldn't offer to haul the battery. I would ask a question when we gathered in the parking lot. Tell me what you drove past to get here; it might take all summer, but it means we begin with the work of naming ourselves.

DWAALLICHTJES

At home, far from where I started out, a map of Amsterdam hangs on my bedroom wall: an urban spiderweb of blue canals and yellow streets strung from the IJ, water that was once the westerly digression of a sea. The paper is starting to tear at the folds. Now I am elsewhere, and I am there, looking at laddered threads of silk that span a ceiling corner, in a room in Amsterdam itself. The spider seems pregnant.

I'd boarded a plane in the evening and landed at sunrise. A dark lens recognized my face. Then came a train aisle jammed with suitcases, a fat rainbow over the varnished harbour, an electronic ticket for a biofuel bus, directions dispensed in the neighbourhood's accent. Yeeaaahh, the sloped man with the scarred chin said, that's right where I live: go back across this bridge, at my street hang a left, turn after the tobacco shop, it's a laundromat now.

The building where I've rented an apartment was once a home for widows and orphans. It has an overgrown courtyard. Red tricycle in the hallway, notice of a tenant meeting, an injured umbrella. A bookshelf with the same book I was reading on the flight. Three girls, daughters of the people who gave me the keys, bounce on the narrow bed. I leave to stay awake.

Brick-walled flats and row houses, street names mounted on their corners, portals lined with Ottoman tiles. An Ethiopian coffee shop where the owner lights a candle on the single table and utters a prayer—for Saint Martin's Day, she tells me. Flower stand, fish market, traffic circle a merry-go-round of bikes. I start to breathe with the breath of the city again. Elstar apples, and rookworst, and the sugared anise served on rusks to celebrate a birth. Gulls carving through November fog. The tiredness that moves in like a wall of fog. I wake up, and Amsterdam is still outside the window. I mistake it for daylight, the streetlight. I lift the curtain and see a passing cluster of children holding lanterns on sticks.

We didn't live here long. Two winters of snowflakes quietly extinguished on the dark green skin of the Noorder Amstelkanaal. Of Amsterdam as home, I would, if I spoke Turkish, use the heard past tense, a conjugation for conveying what we didn't witness or do not recall—like fiction or early childhood or hearsay.

Turkish is a common language in the city. There are shops with fresh pide, baklava, doner, shawarma—*shoarma* when transliterated into Dutch. There's no meat on the spit, so I order the fries in a paper cone. The owner is conversing with a friend who drinks tea from a glass mug, and the only word I understand is *Filistin*, which punctuates the sentences and creaks with grief. To white residents I often look Turkish, but not to the Turkish Dutch themselves.

On the streetcar, a woman in shalwar kameez smiles at me over her daughter's shining hair. In another restaurant, the waiter starts out in Indonesian, then catches himself. When I give the bookstore owner a copy of my book, she grins and says, Your last name is true Amsterdam. Every encounter shifts me in and out of real and imagined belonging.

I was born here. I've returned to study a feeling. A quiet electricity, a blurring of edges between ourselves and our first places. I walk north through the Spaarndammerbuurt. The bakeries, sealed shops in a cold climate, hold their smell of fresh bread close. Then an old factory with a heartbeat. I rise to my toes, press my face to the glass, look in at a sweat-soaked hip-hop dance rehearsal. The window is a mosaic of fractures traversed by the bodies of clouds.

When you live here, your gestures are no longer yours alone; whatever you do becomes part of a project called Amsterdam. *What is my cathedral? I am working on a cathedral that is unknown to me, and by the time it is complete I will be gone and no one will know that I worked on it.* Willem Frederik Hermans, who wrote this in a novel, was born close to the Vondelpark. Former squats, narrow lanes, gracefully tentacled trees. The street is brown and blotched as a Breitner painting. At a bridge that wears its name inside the cast-iron railing, I lean over to spot my head and shoulders in the canal. Fleeting circles fleck the water while a heron hunches on the moss roof of a houseboat, graphite feathers softly ragged from the rain.

Once there were two men lost in a swamp. Their families had been hungry for too long. That blue heron circled down and told them to build their new huts where they stood. Your hamlet, the bird said, will grow into a city that will rule the world. Peat was cut, posts driven down as foundation—13,659 of them still hold up the palace.

Amsterdam, that big city, / It is built on poles; / If that city ever fell over, / Who would pay for that? is a nursery rhyme I was raised with. The question is left hanging, but the answer is pervasive as the damp. Peanut sauce on fries, coffee with a cinnamon wafer. A tall ship named *Amsterdam*, docked at the museum, flying a Dutch East India Company flag. I go to the Oosterpark and find the National Slavery Monument.

I'm shifting my weight to stay warm; what doesn't feel right is the posture of the woman representing freedom. She stands with her spine arched so far back it looks strained. Her shape is a slingshot pulled past breaking. I walk, and through my soles I feel the city's hopscotch pavements. Below them is the hidden infrastructure of its circulations, and then the beams, rusted ship chains, powdered ledgers, busted skulls.

On the Albert Cuyp, I meet an old man in a beautifully dishevelled suit who asks me in Suriname Dutch for a euro. He stares at the ground while I search my bag. Then he murmurs, Such lovely shoes, they grace your feet. To claim belonging here is to harbour a turbulent knowledge in my body: boatloads of people paid for Amsterdam with the substance of their lives. In Banda Aceh, Lampung, Saramacca, Tshwane, Manhattan—in places whose original names are unknown to me because their maps, as if in a nightmare where every figure is the self, are strewn with my own first language.

I used to dream, when I was younger, that I was in an urban square. The powdered, yellow daylight had an indoor quality. There was a wall of tall windows, the outline of a church. It was good, wherever it was. I woke up feeling protected. Every few months this dream recurred.

I returned to the Netherlands one year to visit my great-aunt. She lived in IJmuiden, at the mouth of the canal that goes from Amsterdam to the sea. Whenever I left for the city, she was tense. She pictured the streets as gauntlets of clutching your bag close, refusing insistent offers of hash, averting your eyes from sex workers in storefronts. I'd tell her, I'll be fine—and if she were alive now, I could say, It isn't like that. You do not have to wade through a recumbent crowd outside the station, traversing low vapours of smoke and sweat, swaying on the strings of a guitar song. Your wallet probably won't get stolen, though you will have to empty its digital incarnation for a meal or a bed or a shirt. At the old orphanage, I wash communal dishes with a resident who tells me wistfully, There used to be more birds of paradise.

I ask her what that means.

People who were strange, eccentric, sick or not sick, she says—world inventors! It's so preppy, everyone the same. Look at Zuid, I would never live there now.

On that earlier trip from IJmuiden, I had a backpack, the map that's now taped to my wall, and a scrap of paper with a friend's address. Amsterdam directions: not the First but the Second Constantijn Huygensstraat. I walked from the station to the Dam, and then, as if I'd waded from the shore of consciousness, I found myself inside the dream: phantom church, framed sky, dark paving stones laid in small arcs. *It is a beautiful, large room that everyone may enter* is how writer Renate Rubinstein, whose family fled Berlin before the war, described the square in 1980 during the annual Remembrance of the Dead.

In the dream, I stood on the cenotaph steps: They were wide and shallow and rounded, like wave edges spreading on sand. The square was empty. I was facing the palace and the New Church.

The real square holds a crowd, and a department store named the Bijenkorf, housing an Escherian stack of escalators, and the Hotel Krasnapolsky, after which James Joyce named a shade of red. The palace looks neglected; a white sundial glints from the church. The Dam's name was so comfortably itself to me that I didn't register there was a dam. I had to read it in a book: The remnants of the earliest diversion of the Amstel River are below the square. The New Church was finished in 1408.

That dream held no tension or risk or even narrative. I knew that the doors I saw, any door around the square, would open and receive me. The dream was the feeling of utter trust in a place. *Whenever I get lost,* Phil Hall wrote of his own birth region, *Ontario does not wound me.*

In Zuid I order coffee from a detailed blackboard menu, write in my notebook on a counter of thick wood. I pass a yoga studio, a perfumery, a beauty bar. Then comes the block where my parents lived when rents were ordinary. One short, solid canyon of apartments, an almost covert interval of habitation between larger streets. Straight architectural lines overdrawn with the sinuous branches of French elms. I press my hand to a trunk that the rain has made gleaming and green, and I remember the sculpture by Giuseppe Penone at the Art Gallery of Ontario. Now I can picture the tree's interior: layers of younger, smaller trees nestled inside the present one. Somewhere in us is the plump, exploratory being who tried to bring whatever they touched to their mouths.

Here is the old building number. A door to the right, its golden mail slot below my knees. I wonder what it's so low for. Maybe to separate the inner door handle from a reaching hand or tool. One night in the heard past, my father looked out the window and noticed an idling truck, then saw hurried men lift an entire rack of bicycles into the back. On the left, a stone staircase rises from the stoop to other front doors. It has a wide wooden banister, red brick walls. I imagine the stroller being pulled up backward, away from daylight, the thump on each riser heralding the approach to home. Then a terrazzo landing. Tiles on the wall, square ones, green and pink. Metal nameplates with cursive inscriptions, three buzzers for three apartments. This one. I press my face to the glass, make out carpeted, winding stairs. Quieter stroller wheel thuds, the smells of cooking and sleep. Places are ours, and then they lock to us again.

I ring the buzzer. Through spikes of static, a young voice says she'll ask her mother, then tells me it's not a good time.

Thank you for asking, I say.

It feels right for the flat to remain a closed summit, immune to interrogation. My mother said she placed a mirror in the narrow kitchen so I could watch her from a chair. I still have a picture taken on the balcony out back. My father is three quarters of a smiling face, and I'm beaming in an eyelet dress. Billowed diapers on the clothesline. The horizon, another brick building, is tilted as if the whole city might be a ship on the waves.

A teenager in a denim jumpsuit takes an efficient selfie in front of van Gogh's *The Potato Eaters*, the painting of a room where an oil lamp with a thorned, lopsided flame hangs from a rafter. Amsterdam's a city of good lighting. Windows glow with warmth; they frame fixtures of pleasing designs. Lit orbs are woven into the trees, and alleys are strung with bulbs of soft yellow. At night in the fog, their light is like small clouds of pollen.

Dwaallichtjes, little wandering-lights, are the bluish luminosities that rove over bogs. Folkloric knowledge held that they made skipping motions because they were the souls of unbaptized children. People were warned not to whistle and never to follow. I read this as a child, in a heavy book, and closed it hard. We leave, almost all of us do: for the radiant apparition of opportunity or love or survival itself. And do places remember us after?

At home, I was taking an online course. One night I hadn't done the readings and was drawing on a legal pad, slowly growing lost to the discussion on the screen. Then I heard someone say, Holland is not what I pictured and I'm not sure I'll ever get used to it. My breath caught. I am still learning to live in Holland, a voice from another square said, and her face looked pained. The weather isn't great, but I can wear a raincoat. A third participant shrugged, Everyone wants to go to Italy, but Holland has its own vibe. I started to grasp that the reading I'd missed was an allegory for accepting disappointment. I stayed quiet. To say that I was born in Holland would only sound like metaphor, and clarification would make it funny. And I wasn't born in Holland but in Amsterdam.

In other parts of the country, people sometimes disown the capital city. It's not really Dutch, they say, meaning not homogenous, conservative, reserved. I am visiting during a national election. The atmosphere holds the tension of people hitched to a collective process. That question of how to live together. The government has fallen, an odd word for a voluntary resignation. The trouble was that the ruling party no longer wanted the families of refugees to follow their loved ones to the Netherlands. Cabinet minister

Dilan Yeşilgöz-Zegerius had raised public alarm saying thousands of cases per year, when the real average was seventy. The governing factions couldn't settle this invented matter of funding the reunion of traumatized parents and children. I read this and thought of how, when I was in grade school, the province of Flevoland was added to the maps we coloured in class; it was a sea that had been drained and converted to farmland. Now the country of that enormous effort was claiming a logistical defeat.

In the heard past, my mother wanted children and my father didn't. He said we wouldn't belong anywhere, and she said the world was changing. My possible parents were students. The idea of me floated between them through streets that were for and against. The city allowed squatters to occupy distinguished dwellings but prohibited Dutch citizens of Suriname background from living in certain neighbourhoods. The two groups organized together against segregation and unaffordable housing. Moroccan and Turkish men, recruited north to labour for low wages, received deportation orders, which led to sustained protests for migrant rights. Queer culture dwelled in public spaces. At the Hilton, a famous interracial couple made a performance of their love. It was the city that conceived me first. When my parents brought me home, their Jewish landlady had a small bracelet made, gold with my first name in cursive, spelled almost right.

Yeşilgöz-Zegerius was born the same year I was, in Ankara; her family fled after the Turkish Armed Forces took over the country in 1980. Now she has replaced the former Dutch prime minister as party leader. She could become the first woman and person of colour to lead the Netherlands. I pass her image on transit shelters, in leaflets, on televisions hanging from the grease-coated walls of snack bars: the trick of representation as progress.

The far-right party, in the wake of the controversy, is gaining ground. I trust the city not to elect them, but I don't know about the rest of the country. A friend texts me an afterthought to a conversation. When we were children and lived in the same Dutch town, a boy told my brother to go back to Turkey, and my brother said, You were probably born closer to Turkey than I was. The heard past has found me, and in the early darkness, my phone glows through my pocket. My brother was born in Nairobi. I picture the neighbourhood boy as a man in a voting booth, marking in red pencil the circle for the party that seeks to ban mosques and Qurans. I am tired of remembering his humanity, and afraid of what it would mean to stop. When the streetcar comes I step into air warm with breathing, coats brushing coats, and cannot read anyone's mind.

Places teach you how to move. You start out clumsy, flailing in eager repetitions, until the willed action occurs. Crawling on linoleum floors, over the raised thresholds between rooms. A small, groping hand finding that the radiator is hot. Amsterdam means being lifted onto the front of your mother's bicycle, grinning into the weather, the city flooding your rudderless, permeable, epiphanic attention and tuning your senses. That street with the rhythm of tree trunks at steady intervals. Grand green sigh of the park. Rasped pulse of a dog's bark. Voices of the market, funk of raw fish, a cold plum pressed into your hand.

On early return trips, Amsterdam meant travelling by train from the east, my brothers ricocheting between seats. Craning my neck for the washed light of the station's ceiling. Walking the paved edge of a canal as if it were a balance beam. Meticulously disassembling a hazelnut pastry at a coffee shop with mirrored walls.

Later visits were from the airport in the west. Lowering the gear of my speech into Dutch. Leafing through books at Athenaeum. Glimpsing the fit of my skirt in shop windows, watery but true to colour in the daylight, precise and shadowed at night. Climbing a steep, narrow staircase to a door with an L-shaped handle, sloped ceilings, a mattress on the floor. Amsterdam is the consideration that others are always nearby.

I rent a bike and feel a double estrangement when the shop worker instructs me on the ring lock in blunt English. Then I ride out through the alley, and I'm fluent again, coasting alongside mallard-coloured water, over the hills of bridges, feeling the velvet rain on my face, lifting my legs to avoid the splash of a puddle. I see someone half-raise her left arm for a turn, poised and casual at once, a concise gesture that relies on the entire choreography of the city and isn't how I signal where I live, strong-armed and emphatic, as if reminding drivers that bicycles exist.

I pause to sit on a park bench, ask the white-haired woman beside me how long she has lived in the neighbourhood. She says she doesn't mean to grumble, but she used to reside on the Singelgracht, and when she walked here, through the Rijksmuseum's central passage, past the Stedelijk and the Concertgebouw, she felt like the richest person on earth. Then the tourists took over: They walk so slowly, they walk on bike paths, they don't understand the rhythms. She emphasizes the last word with her hands and laughs at herself. Now I live in a village where nothing happens, and I drive here every Thursday because I cannot go without.

The city archives are in the former trade centre. Three statues of colonial generals on the facade, the coat of arms with its motto: Valiant, Steadfast, Compassionate. In Amsterdam, I feel the sway between loving a place and resisting the urge to align myself with its collective fictions. On the train one evening, men dressed in bright orange shirts and hats ride beside me, jostling with anticipation, bound for the Johan Cruyff Arena. Their brash nationalism makes me watchful, and I want what they want, for our team to win.

At the Stadsarchief, I ask to view the record of my birth and am referred to a clerk at another computer. He explains that the archive functions on a hundred-year delay—the staff are entering statistics from 1923—but he can show me my registration certificate instead. Within seconds, he turns the screen toward me. A scan of a form dated the day after my birth. My typewritten name, the names of my parents, our street address, as well as the deregistration after we left the city.

A box that says *Vr.* My eye falls to the note on the abbreviation. *Vreemdeling.* Foreigner. *Nationality: Kenyan.* I tell the clerk I had a Dutch passport as a child. He says my parents must have applied for it later, because the father's nationality was the one assigned to children then. He is friendly. I'm still asking the other questions I came for—whether I can see how many children were born that day, or what their names were, which isn't possible in his database—but I also sense a word burrowing into me.

From the archives, it's a short walk to the Dam. Human shapes materialize and vanish in the evening fog. The New Church is closed. I walk its perimeter, pull at each door, notice the sign with the hours. The Old Church then, which is not on the square. I enter the enduring quiet of the nave, a dark granite floor of gravestones I attempt not to tread on, which means tightrope walking along the seams. There are sixty thousand bodies buried here, below the city's oldest building, remains that span eight centuries. I feel a flare in the constant ache over the bombing of Gaza, where the death toll is a third of that number in less than two months.

Some inscriptions here are worn to shadows. Others retain their legibility: a duck, an hourglass with wings, a version of my name. At one end of the space, a small, gilded ship hangs in the air, sails rounded with imaginary wind. It hovers there like an oblique acknowledgment of what made Amsterdam. *Vreemdeling, vreemdeling, vreemdeling.* I love my Kenyan belonging; the document's dissonance is in the notion that we could be foreign where we're born. How we are marked from the start by the contortions that pass for reason when the objective is a closed nation.

The hospital is a hotel now. Corridors a garish red, strewn with Amsterdam's three-cross symbol. The main stairs are the last interior remnant of the original building, the lanky manager tells me.

And do you know who was born here?

Johan Cruyff, I say.

Stone steps, concave with use, percussive under my boots. I have a room with a generic interior where I sleep without dreams. When I raise the blind, the morning behind the glass is dim. At the hospital, children weren't allowed to visit, and after my birth my aunt let her eight-year-old daughter scale the fire escape to wave at me.

I'm restless, concerned that this return to origins will be wasted if it doesn't hold clear meaning, so I gather my dirty clothes. One of the books on my parents' shelves had a title that translates to *Most People Are Friendly*. It was newspaper columns by an Amsterdam writer describing his everyday experience of the city. I was learning to read and had the misconception that books for adults were all factual. When I deciphered that spine, I felt the goodness of the world surge through my body.

The neighbourhood around the hospital feels lived in. The market is not for tourists: stands of fruit, shawls, hot curries, plantain. At the laundromat, the teenager at the counter says he isn't busy and will do the laundry for me. I find a bakery and buy a few nostalgic items—kletskoppen, bokkepootjes—to take home to my daughter. When I mention that, they add a bag of licorice. Outside, as I notice that my boot's lace is untied, a woman with a wooden cane taps my elbow and says in a kind voice, Mevrouw.

Then I'm across the canal from Artis, the zoo, and spot a zebra among synthetic boulders, two giraffe necks over a fence. On my right is a row of houses labelled with the months of the year. Someone is smoking a cigar at the November door. I ask about the names.

Old warehouses, he says, the ships had to tell them apart. He lives in February. When he first moved here from Rotterdam, his father wouldn't speak to him because of the betrayal.

At the Maritime Museum, I tour the ship, and afterwards I look at their website: *Throughout the years, a lot has been said and written about the replica of the East Indiaman* Amsterdam. *What does this ship represent for you? Tell us your opinion below.* I start to type that the hold should not be a playground. That although this model of ship was meant for freight, the hold still evokes a space where captured people suffered unspeakably. There should not be a structure of crates and ropes with a sign inviting children to play. But the text box is too small for me to say enough.

On a walk toward Muiderpoort Station, I pass a doorway with an old stone inscription that says, in Dutch, KEEPING PLACE FOR SMALL CHILDREN: one of the earliest daycares. The sigh of missing my daughter. Throughout this interval in the city, I've felt orbited by girls.

I asked a mother for directions one evening, and she said, This way, and walked very quickly down the dark street, pointing out small landmarks as if I were a tourist, and I let her. Her daughter, holding her hand and almost running, kept glancing back at me. Tight cornrows, round barrettes, a measuring look—yes, the stranger was still following. At the former orphanage, a girl asked, For my birthday can I get two piercings in each ear? and her mother, with an eighties haircut, answered, But you are afraid of that, and the daughter said, When I am nine I will not be afraid. Another child with bottomless brown eyes told me of her swimming lessons. When we did the test of swimming in our clothes, she said, my hood flooded, and I couldn't breathe. Now what if I fell in the water with that raincoat on? I said, If that ever does happen, you will know to take it off and swim. At a museum, my friend's agile wisp of a kid stared at a cubist painting and then slowly nodded her head.

The station platform has a mural, portraits of people who live in the neighbourhood. Elhoussaine and I are the same age. He is a social worker for adolescents. At the start of his inscription: *Born and raised here in East.* For a reeling instant I am looking at my other life, the one of the local continuous. I would have seen the hospital close and turned into government offices and then into a hotel, where I'd never stay because I lived here. I would have known the transit routes by heart. Given poetry workshops to the same teenagers Elhoussaine works with. Taken my daughter to toss scraps of bread at the Oosterpark birds. She lives where she was born. I've watched her raincoated figure at the river near our home, swarmed by gulls and ducks and geese, and she was valiant, steadfast, compassionate. But I know that my imagining rests in infinite underestimations. I wouldn't have this daughter. I might not be a mother or a writer. I might not even be alive.

I am walking, and the city's aggregate aesthetic feels wordlessly familiar as it layers textured walls and tortuous trees, flashes high design, flutters the corner of a hand-drawn *Free Palestine* poster, leads pedestrians under a sudden dome. Heavy wooden planters, abloom with late flowers. Gable stones of a fox with a crab on its tail, a ring of skeleton keys, a ship. A fig tree with green parrots in the branches on a houseboat deck. So much of what is beautiful here originated in the Islamic cultures the far-right party leader has publicly called retarded: every apartment portal's painted tiles, the tulips breathing colour outside all the flower shops, the influence of Indonesian architecture on the movement called the Amsterdam School.

A window with a Turkish lamp in it; the heard past surfaces again. My parents were in a lighting store and parked me in an aisle in my stroller. The saleswoman told them, Your baby said *lamp*! After *mama* and *papa*, that was my first word. Your birthplace is where your light comes on, and you do not see it because it is also what fuels your sight.

I find a small Indonesian-Suriname fusion restaurant. It is as old as I am. I place my order through a window at the back, then take a seat and wait. The rattan, batiks, and houseplants quietly resemble the furnishings of my childhood. On the opposite wall are three clocks affixed to a single metal plate. The hour hands end in a teardrop shape. The minute hands are sleeker. Underneath each clock is a tiny metal frame that holds a label, typewritten, slightly askew, with a capital city: Jakarta, AMSTERDAM, Paramaribo.

Only Amsterdam is in capital letters. It is in a serif font, but the other two names are not. The Amsterdam time is right, while the others—I consult my phone—are not. They aren't even aligned to the same part of the hour. Two real cities, but on this wall, they tick outside the present, wings to the headquarters of here.

I'm staring at the clocks. The sense of a submerged logic at work. I wait and let it cohere, and then I know: unhitched from Amsterdam time, returned to themselves, the cities are free. The server signals, and I receive the meal: saté, bakkeljauw, rice, gomma cookies, and three bright colours of hot sauce in tiny bags tied with elastics.

Then my train is the one to the airport. Commuters assemble on the platform. A sky the colour of tin. I am attempting to be a vessel. This luck of returning to spaces where my earliest self was formed—whatever a birthplace awakens in us, I want to take it with me. I sense it dwelling somewhere at my navel, the Amsterdam feeling, which is a kind of sureness, a faith in my own nature. The city unrolls outside the window like a ribbon near its end.

I feel a lurching inside. How does a furtive bog light move? How will it move at the speed of a plane? I'm fastening a tag to my suitcase. Buckling a seat belt over that feeling. Not speaking much, to stop the feeling from escaping through my mouth. The windows clot with grey. We're in the clouds, the dense centres of clouds whose hems have dragged over Amsterdam all week.

You breathe your first breath there. Droplets of canal water are in it, ancient brick dust, down of a heron's breast. With that gulp of particular air, you make your first sound, a rip in the veil between worlds. Your eyes are unfinished. The cells that read colour and light will take months to calibrate themselves to the fractured glare of snow, the blooming blots of spring in the park, the greys and browns of an interior.

You could already hear, but what you received was viscous, elliptical, submerged, and now sounds rouse you with their clarity and range. Your father sings the azan in your ears and the streetcar bell chimes in.

You were held inside someone, and you want her to hold you again in this bright spaciousness. Your blood is your own now. There was a hole in your heart, and it shuts. But whatever spirits dwell in this place, outside the peripheries of the senses, they had a chance to come in.

The plane is through and no longer shaking. Outside, the scale has changed. The clouds are enormous, pale-walled eruptions of mountains, archways, apparitions, towers that are also avalanches, and we pass them at a crawl. Their peregrine, borderless bodies, infused with spectral beams. Soon enough the hour on my watch is wrong.

THE SINGING BONE

Our bodies converge with consciousness in mysterious gradations. We live acutely in our senses, our skin, in the organs that hunger or thirst or desire. We live in our minds. Bones are buried inside us. They start forming when our mothers may not know of our existence yet, and endure longest after our deaths. To draw them up into sensation, outside of injury or disease, is to pull at our depths.

My maternal grandparents died within a few years of each other. Almost as old as the century, they still lived in their own house when the Berlin Wall fell. Slowly, the effort of getting from bathroom to table and back overcame them. They moved to a nursing home, where the hospital bed and the lack of a kitchen were obscured by the flotsam of their former quarters: lamps with tweed shades, upholstered chairs, a hooked tablecloth, faded books.

Even after the move they remained formidable, presiding quietly over four generations, accustomed to hearing only the formal you. When they'd been married for sixty-five years, the local mayor's office presented them with a bronze plate. My grandmother sat on it most days, to protect it from theft. She was white, and her apprehension worsened when the worker in the room was not. What that meant for us, I couldn't drag into awareness then. But I was uncomfortable around my grandmother; her distrust of a stranger was returned to her from an intimate corner. My grandfather played word games with me, sent rhyming verses for birthdays and other occasions. They wrote us on blue airmail paper, his cursive measured and steady, hers with outbursts of jaggedness. She broke her hip, and in her convalescence phoned and whispered she was waiting for everyone else to sleep; then she would run down the corridor to prove that she still could. She died first. I copied and sent him poems: *a starry heaven as I've never seen / looks down on me at night through all the ages.*

The second funeral was the one I attended. There had been other deaths among our family and friends, ones I absorbed in immigrant abstraction: without the proof of bodies or the gathering of loved ones. Now this single ritual stood for burying them all. It was May in the Netherlands, and it rained in clear, plumb drops. My mind hummed with coffee and jet lag. The chapel's steep roof was made of reeds, an invocation of ancient dwellings, the peat huts of past generations whose unions—ardent, tender, perfunctory, or violent—had issued our lives. Eight grandchildren bore the dark coffin to the grave. This is one of the most significant gestures I have made: lowering the heaviness of my grandfather into the soil where my grandmother was and was not. In life, the notion of the body and the spirit seems a dubious separation of mutually generative forms, but death raises the starkness of a divide. Maybe my grandparents were everywhere and nowhere now or lurked in corners of the rooms where they had died or continued inside each of us. What I knew was that their bodies would be side by side, as if resuming their companionship in bed. They were, I assumed, at rest.

The cemetery was large, established, and shaded with mature trees. Wood resembles bone, outlasting the life that made it. The instruments of bone surgeons—mallets, chisels, saws, and screws—are reminiscent of carpentry. But at the core of a living tree trunk is heartwood, dense and compact, no longer a conduit of fluids, while bones are tunneled with damp factories. The root of the word marrow is the word for brain; they have their fat, gelatinous textures in common, they hold versions of cognition. In bones: homesickness, imprints of what your ancestors knew, and the way you might sense, once or twice in a lifetime, that the phone is ringing with earth-shaking news.

During my medical clerkship, I learned to take bone marrow biopsies. Like all procedures on waking patients, this required a double consciousness, which medicine had historically divided and gendered: to be a humane companion to someone's pain, and to concentrate almost ruthlessly on the mechanics of the action. We'd instruct the patient to lay on their side, the nurse would demarcate and clean an area on their hip, and I would drive a needle with a T-shaped handle into the bone. Sometimes I had to stand on my toes and lean my weight down to get through. The nurse would say kindly to that whimpering patient that it was good to have dense bones.

The small city where that elective took place was new to me: a flat stretch on a river, surrounded by low and darkly wooded hills. On walks, I thought of my two brothers and wondered whether, with grandparents from three continents, we would be bone marrow matches only to each other. The town's river was brown with thick, sediment-laden waters. Marrow, the site of hematopoiesis, through which blood cells—the red sacs of hemoglobin, the small clotting particles, the enveloping shapeshifters, the archival ones that hold the viral markings—are all generated from one pluripotent cell form. The language itself wades into the figurative: in our marrow, there is poesis, and we are plurally potent.

A year after my grandfather's funeral, my middle brother and I were both undergraduate students, and we lived for a while in the same house. It was that awaited phase of spring when the air is mild, and evenings are awash in light. The house was near a park that had been a gravel quarry and was now a deep, square pit of trampled, struggling grass. We'd started playing touch football there with a few friends, and onlookers had joined in, and soon a regular afternoon crew had formed. I liked sports when I could play on my brother's team. When we were children, his presence on the soccer pitch or basketball court had felt like the compensating factor for my own; if I made an inadvertently detrimental move, he could balance it with a stellar play.

One afternoon, the ball was tossed, and three or four players collided as they tried to make the catch. When my brother stood up from the scrum, his hand was pressed against his shoulder, face drawn in pain. Pulling his T-shirt collar aside, he revealed a bump under the skin; the outer end of his collarbone had lifted. The others debated whether this was a tear or a break. One player who drove a taxi said that there was no treatment and he could lend my brother a sling. Another player, freckled and shy, told us her cousin had needed surgery. My brother was unsure of what to do. He'd turned pale and clammy with pain. The hospital happened to be across the street and the sign for the emergency room in plain sight, so I took him in.

The sliding doors opened to a triage nurse at a desk in front of an almost empty waiting room. I started to explain what had happened. She interrupted me to ask if my brother had OHIP coverage. He did, I said, but we had nothing on us—only our water bottles and keys. I asked if she could call our family doctor for the information. She ignored me. I said I could get his card while he waited. She said that he wasn't allowed in the waiting room until we had proof of insurance. I told my brother to wait on a bench in the doorway, and I would run home for his wallet. The nurse said no, he could not stay inside the building. My brother muttered, Let's just go and get it then.

I was never as forgiving as him. I loathed that white nurse with her ashen hair, her scowl. And here was a violence that could turn cyclical, her looking at my brother in his mute pain and turning him away, me wanting to shove the desk into her stomach. But my perspective was one I could have articulated: my brother is hurt, and there are doctors here, so open the goddamn gate. Where did her action arise, past the supposed offense of our status or colour, and could she have named its origins? I didn't ask the nurse, like I hadn't asked my grandmother. They would have had to extract a distortion that was somewhere in their muscles, tense and practised, and hadn't known daylight. There was no instrument for anyone to do it for them. Surely the bones would not harbour that falseness. I had to believe that all of us were first made of a substance we could trust.

I knew I'd cause my brother more discomfort if I argued with the nurse. So as we walked the few blocks home I stewed with silent rage, and we returned with the card and he was grudgingly triaged. The clavicle, slender and wave-shaped, is the last of all our bones to finish growing. On that day, neither of us had quite reached the age of its maturity. His had separated, meaning the ligaments that held it to the shoulder blade had partially let go. The taxi driver was right that he didn't need surgery, only anti-inflammatories and a sling.

I visited my grandparents' grave whenever I was in the Netherlands, every three or four years. Dense spruce boughs behind the tombstones, sparrow chirps, the rightward drone of traffic. A quiet love for two buried presences; the feeling that they were moved to see me. What if the spirit doesn't vacate but locks itself deeper inside the disintegrating body—what if it clings to the particles that comprised us even as they turn to soil or ash?

One day, my mother forwarded an email from her oldest brother. The lease on the grave was expiring, he wrote, and asked his remaining siblings, and the children of those who had died, to vote for or against its renewal. Without a new contract, the remains would be exhumed and placed in a mass grave elsewhere in the cemetery. My uncle was in favour of that option; he named the high rental costs and explained that his own age made him hesitant to assume further responsibility.

I hadn't known it was becoming customary for graves to be rented in crowded cities or countries, and my sense was that the exhumation would be a form of trouble—spiritual trouble. But our family's methods were formal, and the decision lines were clear: I was one generation removed from having input. People submitted their preference in the email thread. Nobody argued. My mother wished for the grave to stay intact, but the vote was three to two against renewal.

I looked at the cemetery website. Loved ones were not permitted to attend a grave's clearing, as it could be upsetting, it said. I pictured an excavator and two men, their rain suits, packed lunches, gravedigger humour. Rags of flesh still clinging to bones. *Besides this*, the website said, *the intense expressions of emotions by the descendants at that time could hinder the persons in performing the activities.* That perspective felt culturally familiar to me. We had conducted the funeral accordingly, without unleashing disruptive emotions: upright and stoic in the pews, blinking down tears at the grave, returning to the chapel to stand in line and nod through serial condolences.

The website noted that what remained in the graves was usually only parts of the deceased's skull and pubic bone. I was skeptical of that. It had only been fifteen years. But what struck me in the emails between my mother and aunts and uncles was that no one mentioned the bodies. The three who wanted to relinquish the grave named the cost and maintenance duties as obstacles; the two who wished to see it preserved liked having a place to visit the dead. In other words, for this half of my family—this cluster of current and former Christians who worked in teaching and publishing and government—ancestral remains held no apparent meaning.

So there was an hour, unknown to me, when the scraps of the two who had made my mother were lifted from the earth and dropped into a hole with nameless others. With that transfer, their earlier internment became symbolic; we hadn't done it for the sake of the bodies themselves, but for the ritual of burial and an interval of visitations to the site. I didn't feel anything as nameable as sadness, but the practicality of the operation was unsettling.

'The Singing Bone' is a story that recurs in a range of cultures. I grew up with a version contained in a volume of Grimm.

Once upon a time, there was a man who killed his brother and buried him under a bridge. Many years later, a shepherd was crossing the bridge with his flock, and he noticed a small, white bone on the bottom of the creek below. He carved it into a mouthpiece for his horn. When he next blew on the horn, the bone began to sing of its own accord. It sang in the voice of the slain brother and told of his murder.

When I was in medical school, every first-year student was loaned a bone box from the anatomy department. It was a rectangular wooden case with a hinged lid, holding the loose bones of as complete a skeleton as possible. At home, I sat at my table and held the ribs, observing the difference between the ones that had been anchored to the sternum with cartilage, that substance now brown and hard, and the ones that had floated. I laid out the radius and ulna beside each other and tried to recreate their rotation. I traced the grooves and openings for major blood vessels and nerves. Bones were clean to work with. The gruesome stage was over. Arranging them on the floor, I got the impression of a small adult body.

A while after signing out the bone box, I had a vivid dream. In it, I awoke in my bed and heard the presence of someone on the other side of the sliding panel that marked off the living room side of the apartment. I felt a sense of clarity and terror. I thought of a burglar, but then realized the sound I was hearing was the turning of newspaper pages. Someone was reading the Saturday paper that I had left on the table. Not a burglar but a ghost. I forced myself to get up and face them, walking through vortices thicker than air. Pushing the panel aside, I froze: the bone box levitated near the ceiling. In the morning, I wrapped the box in a shawl, carried it to school, and returned it to the anatomy lab.

What I heard of those bones was unbidden, but there are people who do the meticulous, scientific work of listening. In *The Bone Woman*, Clea Koff writes of her experiences as a forensic anthropologist exhuming mass graves in Rwanda and the Balkans. How the effort starts with locating sites, seeking out local reports of what happened or indications of disturbed earth. Then digging to uncover the remains, cleaning them in place as well as possible so that they can be photographed. Lifting each body and moving it to an examination tent or shelter. Determining age through the fusion of plates within the bones or the eruption of molars, and sex through the shape of the pelvis. Documenting whether the corpse was exposed for long or buried right away. Marking the evidence of trauma. Extracting mitochondrial DNA to determine blood relations.

Those excavations were meant to repair a rupture. The evidence could lead to processes of justice, and the remains could be given proper burial by loved ones. After reading, I wondered how a collective grave like the one where my grandparents were buried might look to future forensic anthropologists. They would find cluttered pockets of eroded bones, unceremoniously deposited, most of them identifiable as belonging to elderly adults. There would be no signs of systematic violence. Mass graves usually represent massacres, plagues, or other disasters, but here the trouble was a lack of space—or a prioritization of what space was for: not the dead, but new roads and office parks and garbage dumps. And what provisional formulations would scientists make then, about the people who willingly handled their ancestors with construction equipment?

There is a Muslim cemetery in downtown Nairobi, near the crowded Kariokor market, and my paternal great-grandfather was once its keeper. He lived inside the walls with his wife and children, rode a motorcycle with a sidecar around the grounds, took his grandchildren for reckless joyrides under fruit trees that he cultivated. The newly deceased were ritually washed by family members of the same sex, dressed in white shrouds, and buried on their right side, facing Mecca: an image of magnetism, of collective sleep. He led the prayers, kept the records, maintained the graves with their plain white stones.

There was no Islamic cemetery in the Netherlands when we lived there, but my father, in his unadorned delivery, let us know of certain rules. We bury the dead as soon as possible. We do not burn them. We mourn for forty days. We do not walk on graves.

On the maternal side, both burial and cremation were options, a choice to be conveyed discretely through a notarized document. In my restlessness after my grandparents' exhumation, I consulted the Bible, which they had read from after every supper. There was the passage where Joseph instructed his family that when the time came to leave Egypt, they should unearth his bones and bury them again at their new home. And one where the prophet Ezekiel, in the Valley of Dry Bones, performed a resurrection: *And as I was prophesying, there was a noise, a rattling sound, and the bones came together, bone to bone.* I asked my mother if her parents had knowingly signed a lease for a grave, but she wasn't sure.

I read about other death rites, including the ones that rely on vultures. Zoroastrians have traditionally used small towers on which the dead are arranged in concentric circles. After vultures consume the soft parts of the bodies, the bones are left to bleach and dry, then moved into a pit in the centre of the tower. Lime is added, and rain slowly washes the decomposing bones through several filters, until their residue flows out to a river or sea. The vultures are said to possess a mystic eye that helps the soul make its cosmic transition.

This form of burial is less common than it used to be, partly because vultures are now endangered in India. Their disappearance had to do with the same kind of anti-inflammatory medication my brother took for his shoulder. The drug was widely given to milk cattle, and when vultures ate the corpses of those cows, the residue was fatal to them.

In the absence of the birds, the human bodies rotted instead of being swiftly stripped to the bone. In Mumbai, some towers were amended with the installation of solar concentrators that would speed decomposition of the bodies. The story could be a contemporary fairy tale, a warning that there's no such thing as an isolated action.

I started walking on graves some years ago. I live near a park whose colonial history is that it used to be a Christian cemetery. An estimated ten thousand people were buried there before it closed in 1865. The city had acquired the land and envisioned a park. Families were given time to exhume the bodies of their loved ones and reinter them elsewhere, but there were obstacles, including the money required for the transfer and the difficulty of locating each grave precisely. And surely there were those who, as I did a hundred and fifty years on, felt reluctant for otherworldly reasons. The Other World is what my paternal grandmother calls the place where the dead are.

In the park, approximately one tenth of the bodies were moved; the others remain, unmarked except for where the worn edges of one or two gravestones protrude from the grass. Their bones still accidentally surface sometimes: when one of the bordering streets was under repair, my friend found a jawbone in the gravel. There are local stories of children, sixty or seventy years ago, riding bikes with skull trophies on their handlebars.

Skeleton Park, as it is widely called, has shaped for me how it feels to dwell where the dead are buried. I've done so much there: waited, nursed, celebrated, kissed, argued. I've gone inside books, shared meals, listened to concerts. Had hundreds of conversations. Spotted the first April robins, watched bats agitate between the trees at night. I've been vastly ordinary: preoccupied, distracted, forgetful. Pushed the swing, the swing, the swing, that tolling pendulum. And at every instance, the dead have been there, as a sort of undertow, a silent crowd whose remains encounter the seasons only through the slowly fluctuating life of the soil. They're not my dead, but their presence makes a difference. They alter the light: I've never found the same light in other parts of the city, light that seems almost a substance as it pours between the maples, colours the grassy spaces, or fractures itself on falling snow. I am aware of being given something. The gulp of cold water on a scorching day, the sight of a child's incandescent grin, the mutterings of a frightened person in a sleeping bag; in the park, perceptions that would feel unanchored elsewhere somehow gain gravity as parts of the same continuous narrative.

My brother and I have played pick-up soccer there and eaten takeout noodles and debated political diversities of tactics. We inhabit a strange phase now; we're far from the graves of our ancestors, which are dispersed on separate continents, and have buried no one in the new country. An interval like a held breath. In the meantime, the last fragments of our maternal grandparents have been lifted and dropped. I don't know the consequences, or even whom to ask; any answers live in us now, in a singing of the marrow, below the noise of thought. We have altered the earth and so will have to continue to reinvent our death rites. And I will carry the discord of those bones like a remainder in long division: a genealogy of downward figures, a reckoning that doesn't quite work out.

SPIRIT MATERIALS

When I find the envelope in the mailbox, its soft heft differs from a paper letter. Sweet arrival, another trapeze leap caught. For three years now, Amy and I have written to each other in embroidery. Our conversation explores faith: her Jewish origins, my Muslim and Christian ones, and how we hold them in the present. We were students when we met. We postered the campus with lyrical protests, brewed herbal remedies, and read on her apartment's fire escape until dusk. As urgently as spring meltwater, in elated and troubled bursts, we were releasing what we had been told, and examining what was left. Since then, we've lived provinces apart while cultivating our creative practices in parallel, Amy as a visual artist. When we last saw each other, we were both considering the mystical traditions of our inherited, half-discarded faiths. Amy had worked in embroidery before, and I was reading poems of questions and answers. So, we merged where we'd been and what we wanted to find out into a mutual undertaking.

Amy started with one embroidered question for me: *when someone asks your religion, what happens internally?* It came as the leaves were falling. I stitched an answer and another question, and sent them to her. And so it goes. Her thread is red and mine is blue. We work on strips of near-white cloth, approximately as tall as a pen, often wider than the span of our arms—mine are torn from an old bedsheet, boiled in tea to take out the harsh glare—and then we mail them between Nova Scotia and Ontario by affordable, unregistered mail; a gesture of faith embedded in the process. Someday, we'll sew the fragments together and the conversation will be longer than a skein of geese.

///

A line of geese in flight resembles a row of running stitches. If it were, there would also be a goose in every gap, but on the reverse side of the sky's fabric. The bird thread moves; its lagging end isn't knotted, and the leading one follows an invisible needle that darts in and out of the cloth. Skilled stitches are evenly spaced, and of the same tension as the backing material. Is that how a migrating goose feels, at one with the weave of the air?

Our words are done in backstitch, a strong stitch that moves two lengths forward, one length back. This choreography requires more hours and thread than the running one, but it makes an unbroken line, thin and smooth on the front of the fabric, more ragged on the back where each stitch is doubled. The script is cursive, so both the thread and letters form lines that return in looped increments to where they've been and then continue forward. When I write, my mind moves like that—rereading the last sentence, pulling ahead into a new one.

On the fabric, I first write my phrases in pale blue ink, and then follow the line with the needle. Is that sure path what makes me feel so held and settled when I stitch? Or maybe it's the slowing down, the pliant and tactile words that surface outside the rapids of speech or texting or typing or writing by hand. Initially, whatever mood I'm in persists, subtly evident in the length and tension of the stitches, the tiny, tell-tale holes left when my aim is untrue. But then there's a shift. I am doing this with my fingers, with elementary technologies, the lightly rhythmic repetition of uncomplicated motions, and I start to admire the dark blue line that forms in their wake. It is steady. It has a good shape. The feeling is praise. I am quietly praising the line's unfolding existence to myself, and then the sensation circles outward, to the room, to the constellations of what surrounds me.

///

The lines of our embroidery are at rest, but contain an elapsed movement. *A line has time in it,* painter

David Hockney has said. An opening, a closure—we locate them in our lives, and then find the ends of the thread are frayed: When did I begin this embroidering? In answering Amy's stitched question, or twenty-five years earlier at our first hello, or in florals across the knees of my grade ten jeans, or on a stiff white plastic grid, with clumsy and deliberate kindergarten hands? Perhaps it was longer ago, a gesture that could germinate again in my body because my grandmothers had made it, as had theirs, and theirs—by the light of a flame, chewing a scrap of tobacco.

Other starts and stops are ingrained in my materials. The cotton grew in Egyptian fields sprayed with toxins that teenagers carried in cannisters on their backs. My sewing bag is made from fabric that a friend gave me, printed with a dictionary of words in a shorthand invented in 1888; the notation for *start* looks almost like a downward crawling snail, and *stop* like a cursive r. That same friend made a brown felt pocketbook to hold my needles; it shuts with a magnetic little click.

///

What I've learned so far is to begin, as with prayer, by washing my hands. To lay the blank cloth on the table, not the floor with its nails and seams. To write my words in fabric marker ink that will later vanish in seconds under the tap. To buy the good, eighteenth-century brand of embroidery floss because others don't have the same lustre, and break off. To split its six strands and use two at a time. To watch for any deviation from the intended line, because what seems minor and concealable will soon alter the entire course—therefore, to resist the lure of progress and pause to free the needle, use its tip to undo the errant stitch, and rethread its narrow eye. To locate dormant pockets in the schedule of my hands—the intervals of phone conversations or online meetings or sitting with a morning coffee out on the wooden porch steps—when they can be writing with thread. I tried to work on the porch in the rain once, under a sheltered edge, but some drops struck the fabric and caused such quick erasures that I lost the line.

Rain looks like running stitches when we watch it falling close to us; a fastening of sky to ground with water threads. From far away, a raincloud appears to wear a gauzy skirt of greys. My eyesight is not the same as when Amy and I first became friends, when I wanted only June's long sunlit days. The needle's little void has blurred. I have softer, broader vision now; every weather lives in it.

///

Shorthand is a compression, a tool for writing when the words are coming fast. What if longhand meant an elongation, an elaboration of regular handwriting? I'd want to learn that script, where the intake of breath before a word is also part of the word, where even the sound of one letter falling into another has its own shape. I could use it to overcome what I dread—that I will find I have withheld myself, haven't conveyed how deeply I love whom and what I love. In narrative, to embroider is to add fictional details, but Amy and I are asking each other to be plain. *When do you feel belonging? What in this world belongs to you?*

Embroidery on cloth is an embellishment: its presence suggests that there was enough, of minutes and material and skill, to give them over to beauty. Evidence of some degree of peace. The small round mirrors that one grandmother sewed onto my shalwar kameez; the smocking that the other stitched into the front of my summer dress. We too are lucky to have space for this slow work, but our purpose isn't to decorate the fabric. Questions of the spirit seem almost ornamental when life is untroubled, and then become essential when it's not. This crawling medium magnifies the visual and temporal weight of their asking. It takes the hedging out of my answers. If I make a mistake, I bleed.

Time is a line, and in our ancestries it is a tree, and in experience it is elastic. Once, I was standing in farmland in spring, and a gunshot sent up a flock of resting geese. They scattered in pulsed circles from one midpoint, like the puddle's surface after a raindrop: another expression of how time functions.

The women who made me were centres from whom prayers and philosophies and skills moved outward. Not all of them were literate, but they possessed great knowledge; I feel it lurking tidally inside the quiet sewing hours. Some practised the Punjabi art of phulkari, using the darn stitch to pattern shawls for the dowries of their daughters leaving home, while others, on the North Sea coast, cross stitched fine initials into their sons' sweaters, for identification if they were lost at sea. I sense the devotion imbued in those needlework gestures, whose makers might find me a lapsed inheritor, doubter of scriptures, moving slowly through elementary stitches—though I can also imagine them in spirited conversation with Amy and I, over cups of tea, into the night. Maktub, *it is written,* is the Islamic metaphor for fate. A stricture when I at first confused it with an inescapable course of life, but wise when I picture it now as love's pale, ephemeral marker line, and our living itself as the thread that follows, strays, returns.

DRAWING LINES

After the lobby's cursive ramp, Sarindar Dhaliwal's show would be on the ground floor: *When I grow up I want to be a namer of paint colours*. The gallery worker smiled at me as if in recognition and scanned my phone so quickly it looked accidental—a sleight of hand that seemed to turn the ticket to formality. Now I would be quieter, restrained in movement, without water. Museums, like poetry readings, can make for awkward encounters with art.

The right wall of the corridor held a long banner photograph of upright pencil crayons laid snugly against each other, larger than life, grouped in colour gradients. Pleasure, a broad grin, weathered teeth of living. The impression that dragging a xylophone mallet along the image would sound out a scale. There was a barrier: a low rope. The pencils, whether hexagonal or round, tall or worn to stubs, were almost all sharpened, a chromatic vocabulary primed for use. That work was called *Southall:*

Childplay. The brand name from my own childhood, Bruynzeel, was on some stems.

We map out rote temporalities and may mistake them for living—the exhibition starts in July, the city is two and a half hours away, the gallery opens at 10:30, the overnight is at my friend's apartment, I'll get something at the gift shop for my daughter who returns on Friday—until somewhere inside the sequence, diffusely when out in the world, and concentrated when embedded in an artwork, comes that detail, the pinprick opening through which the fabric of time tears apart. We have to let ourselves be ambushed. For instance, by a seventh or eighth birthday and the flat tin box with its two octaves of colour, the teeth-gritting wish to not be forced to share it with brothers, and the focused labouring over a copy of the image on the lid (butterflies above a grassy meadow), which is an apprentice impulse and a gesture of return: Thank you parents I am a good child I have drawn you a pretty picture.

Prettiness has a different purpose in the exhibition. Not a defusing or decorative offering, but a dual alchemical method. Southall was the British town of Dhaliwal's immigrant childhood, and also a racist concept: *There was this idea,* she wrote, *that it was becoming a ghetto of Pakis or whatever word they used.* Aesthetic beauty is an invitation for outsiders to enter the difficult material, while allowing initiates to experience its transformation. *This function,* artist Rajni Perera writes of Dhaliwal's work, *is made by us and for us.* I turned to the opposite wall and saw my mother tongue, a row of words that start with zed and mean: very (also sore), sweet, soft, sour, seeds. The backdrop was painted images of pears and apples, a section of a map. Dhaliwal had also lived in Amsterdam. The next work, in English, was a kind of fairy tale about an egg on the street at King and Maitland in Kingston, which was the corner where the library books that I'd left on the roof of the car when I buckled my daughter in had avalanched onto the windshield. Soon I was in a kaleidoscope of origins, luminous, hypnotically familiar, but askew enough to be revelatory. The rooms held the vivid colours of my father's culture, our clothes and architecture, our language that was opaque to me. Was the effect that my existence expanded, or that I perceived its real dimensions? Either way, some boundary moved. I was less alone, aware that my ruts of selfness were taking place within wider, livelier thoroughfares.

The show's title piece consisted of small rectangles of colour, named playfully and obliquely: *moss green* and *leaden sea rain* for three shades of pinkish beige, *fiery mars* followed by *fairy maize.* An equivalent deliciousness of words and shades whose quiet collisions upended notions of expectation, perception, and meaning.

In the last room was the map, the photographic one of Pakistan and India and Bangladesh that's made of marigolds, called *the cartographer's mistake: The Radcliffe Line.* I faced the image and could feel the resonance: after the blazing trains, curved blades, the harrowing raids and radiant escapes that my childhood nightmares somehow knew to conjure, the geographic confusion and dendritic migrations of my father's stories, we may be given a map resurging with sacred flowers, the colours of blood and fire channeled into soft, fringed petals, a healing vibrancy, because whatever it is in our psyches that registers an injury is also what receives the beautiful.

I longed much too physically for what I found beautiful, the Amsterdam writer Etty Hillesum wrote, *I wanted to have it.* To sustain the feelings the work had stirred, to conjure them again at will, I bought the postcards and the catalogue of an older exhibition, a bright orange hardcover lettered in gleaming fuchsia. In this too lived the composite effect of the aesthetic. What one kind of viewer could plunder, another could harbour. I understood how artist Pamila Matharu, who as a child had reluctantly helped her mother plant marigolds, felt after seeing Dhaliwal's map: *I came home that evening and looked at my walls long and hard. I knew in my body, mind and spirit that I was going to give that artwork a home.*

My version of this was the wish to ask the artist about her experiences in Amsterdam, and her writing practice, and her work with the concept of the Akashic Records. A curator at the local gallery where I worked part-time knew Dhaliwal, and when I mentioned my questions, she sent an email of mutual introduction. Dhaliwal answered, and we started to schedule a conversation, but then I didn't hear from her; because of the show, her calendar was very full.

This gallery where I worked was small enough for the role to be twofold—reception and security—and large enough to hold an international collection. Reception meant welcoming and orienting the public, answering the phone, handling the mail and parking passes. Security was disarming and arming the alarm system, counting the number of visitors in the four-and-slash notation of prisoners counting days, monitoring them through closed circuit cameras, patrolling the spaces hourly and filling out a checklist. The front desk was never to be vacant, so two people covered each shift. They could split the job into its halves, but often the tasks overlapped.

In a corner of the desk, hidden behind the counter, was a screen divided into twelve or sixteen boxes: the atrium, the loading dock, the galleries from multiple angles, all in grainy greyscale, streaming live. I'd know the number if I had watched them enough. The cameras were supposed register movement, but the sensors didn't work well. Clicking on a view blew it up. The policy was that if there were any visitors in the gallery, they had to be observed. On a chair with clever little wheels, I pulled myself to the screen, located the human figures, identified them as the ones who had come in the doors, though they had lost their colour and their faces. Their movements were less fluent than in life. Some disappeared into a blind spot, emerging from the corner of another box. The minutes slowed. Past the tedium was a tenser discomfort; I was wrestling inside the shirt of a feeling and couldn't find the openings.

A year before the gallery job, I'd been at Museum London for a show. I wanted to spend a while with one painting and that area had no bench, so I sat on the floor. When I left, the worker at the desk asked how my visit was; I said good, and he said, My own favourite painting of hers is the one of the waves.

You were watching me! a student exclaimed at our gallery in amused condemnation. He had leaned over the desk to retrieve his phone that we were charging, and seen the monitor. I wondered if the hitch was that I was watching, the one who greeted him, or that anyone was. Our initial conversation had raised a small contract of trust. If I had so little faith in it, what was it for? At the screen I tried to take a narrow view; I looked only for violations. Not so much for thefts or heists, as I had imagined before the training, but for any touching of the art, accidental or otherwise.

Those two won't, I'd tell myself, they can't reach the wall from that bench. And not that group, the docents are with them, so they're already being watched. And he won't either, his caution was clear from the outset, hands on his back while leaning for a closer look. I justified looking away, reading a line or two in a book. Alright, that one touched, but instantly recoiled as if the work was made of fire, because the sensation recalled for them the rule. True, the one who affirmed my reciting of the reminder that even the textile art should not be touched was now running her palm over a meticulously restored tapestry, her grown daughter tugging at her arm. I too have imagined my exceptionalism, deeming my own minor action to be harmless, when I know that collectively we are the starlings plastering Rome.

The prohibition was clearer than the consequences. A first level of intervention was to patrol the gallery, distinguished by our walkie-talkies, our presence serving as deterrent. Then there was telling the visitor not to touch the art. If they persisted, an experienced co-worker advised, we could add that there were laser alarms in the frames that disrupted our work at the desk—but I knew I wouldn't, because I'd raised a toddler and recognized my limits on the disciplinary bluff. The hourly security walk-through, for its movement, for its survey of the art, felt like a break. But the gaze was active and selective: check that lights are working, glass cases are clean, windows shut, floors clear, benches in place, works of art unmoved. It was a form of looking that, I suspect, aligns with what some people mean when they refer to the real world. Property, money, order. At the end of my rounds, I would pause in front of a lithograph, *Owl of the Sea* by Kenojuak Ashevak.

Of Inuktitut, I have read that she said, *There is no word for art. We say it is to transfer something from the real to the unreal.*

I lack the linguistic and cultural context to know her meaning, but the phrase feels generative in me. This owl is a bird with wings of seaweed and a fish-tail, watchful, over waves of frigid blue. For a moment I receive what there is no word for, then bow lightly to thank her, very lightly because I know that I'm on camera.

At the gallery, I felt lucky to work at a human scale where the director might pitch in with hauling tables out for an event. During the autumn of working there, I was also fortunate to visit the Rijksmuseum in Amsterdam. I arrived at a side door, where three uniformed staff were on duty. One scanned my phone, confirming that I had a reservation but would need to pay inside. Not everyone in the lineup did: they'd paid online or held annual passes. I went in, passed more guards, descended a wide staircase, found my bearings among loose clusters of visitors in the glass-roofed atrium, looked at the cafe that hovers over the giftshop—then a guard approached with a nod of greeting, extending his arm to direct me to the ticket booth across the hall. An operation where all guests were tracked; surely every frame was rigged with a laser alarm. Rembrandt's *The Night Watch* was scaffolded for restoration work. A small crowd, like a disbanded and distracted version of the group inside the painting, took pictures of the empty elevator platform. That surgical privilege of conservators, permitted to touch the art.

It may have been at the Rijksmuseum, as a child, that I was first told not to touch artwork. A rule is conveyed and we make it our own. We raise the surface tension of our bodies to comply. I do recall a field trip in Toronto after I'd already integrated the warning. And I thought I still knew the exhibition's name, and the gallery, and the painting, and what grade I was in, but now that I've searched I know this was an impossible configuration of separate memories; there was an incident that generated a feeling, the feeling possessed a gravitational field, which slowly pulled in the moons of these facts. The grade is right, because I can picture the teacher, whose stubble gave his patient face a shadowed look, telling me there were some great painters where I was from.

In my childishness, I thought of it as one word, greatpainters, the artist Hedda Sterne once said.

I still took people's word for things, still felt a seasick awe at downtown skyscrapers, and could be thrown into incomprehension and heartbreak over a human asleep on a grate. If someone said, This is a very important collection of paintings, then I would view the paintings not only as objects, images, small worlds, but as a definition of importance. What a perilous stage of life.

We were released into the gallery, and I stopped first at a painting of a girl who was staring at the room. Another girl, a real one, was drawn to it as well.

Look, she said, and pointed a finger right into the figure. The canvas billowed out to its frame and my mouth froze in an O—the glory and alarm of watching the forbidden surface move. A guard rushed over to reprimand us.

I said emphatically, I know.

The other girl shrugged. I didn't know her, and it wasn't a dream, she wasn't the part of me that longed to be immune to censure, but I envied the shrug and the turning of her back. Her touch had seemed a miscalculation of distance. Now the spark of however the art had intrigued her was effectively doused.

For a while, around that age, I had a small belief about touching things with the pads of my fingers. I felt the release of a smudge of myself, an electric sort of presence that I left on surfaces. It was disconcerting to lose this interior part of me that would remain exposed and vulnerable. The remedy was to touch the same surface with my nail, which neutralized the loss. The feeling never occurred at home, but it did at other houses, and was potent in public places like an office building with a metal banister along its stairs—long touch in motion was the worst. Touching mattered too much to refrain from altogether: it was a form of being aware. Fortunately, the fingernail trick was efficient, requiring only a quick tap, anywhere on the touched object. Though if I had accidentally made contact with a painting, I would have understood the rule: that was an irretrievable emission.

A thin wedge of translucent memory, unsearchable in any records: I'm in the atelier of a friend's mother, Florine, and her boyfriend. She is a painter and he a sculptor. The word *atelier*, its magnetism: there are spaces that exist for making art, the materials live there, dream objects and phrases hang on the walls. My friend finds it boring, so his mother takes me on my own. Today there is a dark stone sculpture, cat sized, rounded and with a hollow.

May I touch it? I'm otherwise too shy to speak, but these words come out.

Of course, the boyfriend says, and beams at Florine: see, it makes people want to touch!

My palm on the stone. Cold, smooth, curved, resolute, solemn, hibernating, swimming, loud, clairvoyant, homesick. The staggering concept of infinity.

In *Touching the Art,* Mattilda Bernstein Sycamore writes of bringing her hand to a marble sculpture in the garden at the Baltimore Museum of Art and being told by a staff member to stop: *And the truth is that as soon as this person tells me I can't touch the sculptures, all the sculptures become ugly.*

One winter afternoon there was an email from Sarindar Dhaliwal. She would be in the city for a residency in the spring and I could interview her then.

My walk to see her took me past a place where I had lived. I glanced up at the bay window. *Western chromophobia* was a phrase first used by David Batchelor; I had read it in an essay on Dhaliwal's work by MJ Thompson. A few days earlier, someone had described to me how it felt to move to Canada from Mexico: Suddenly, no colour.

Now I heard the memory of a siren. During my year in that apartment, the downstairs neighbour was a heavy smoker who rarely left home. Yellow vapour hovered in the kitchen cupboard under my sink. I left saucers of vinegar there. When the neighbour cracked his kitchen window open, smoke poured into the alley, and based on its volume I pictured him not only chain-smoking but inhaling from several cigarettes at once. Winter in that neighbourhood was a grey sky, grey street, grey houses—but two or three times, a passerby called the fire department, and when the wailing, pulsing truck pulled up, that was the arrival of colour, the remembrance of red, and I would stare down at its fierce and saturated warmth and feel the quickening of my blood, and allow that the smoker and I had made a fair trade that day.

I hung my wet raincoat on a hook at the inn, and then Dhaliwal was saying hello. She wore grey clothes accented with vivid pink and yellow. We sat in a room with an empty fireplace. I wonder if there's tea, I thought.

I asked for tea, Sarindar said, but they only have ice water.

I poured it from the jug into our glasses and took out my notebook. Sarindar had lively, wary eyes.

What I was working on came out in evasions: not a profile, not for an art journal, won't really know until I'm writing. I told her I admired the concision and rhythm and understatement of the title *the cartographer's mistake*, and did she recall how she first thought of it?

She didn't answer that directly, but described planting an actual map of marigolds for an earlier exhibition. Then she told me of her work in a factory outside of Amsterdam, and hitchhiking through Europe and Asia. Sarindar was a good storyteller, but the recounting sounded practised, and I had already read the same things in articles or interviews. Our conversation, over two mornings, didn't truly become one. Her own evasion, when I tried to interject with a question, was to say with the mischievous smile of someone who knows her hiding places, Sorry, I'm not making much sense.

But it did make sense: I was a stranger with a nebulous project.

What I saw was the determination it had taken to become an artist. Some of what Sarindar encountered had lessened for my generation: her art had been called decorative and craft. A professor had told her, Maybe you should be a seamstress. Other elements were ones I recognized: the struggle to make a living, the constant fluctuation between working artistically and administratively. There was no indication that these aspects got easier; she was, to any lurking child in me, a mother figure of some warning. I understood her long comet streak of defiance: she had left home at sixteen, gone to art school in England, changed the spelling of her name, insisted even in her early work on the significance of her own frames of reference.

In art she dissolved material and economic limits, painting the lush gardens she longed for but didn't have, making herself the proprietor of an adjacent, imaginary hotel. Her works invoked a colonialism with consequences, ones that were not only painful and tragic, but also awaiting her bright subversions. She inverted her own restrictive schooling into a teaching philosophy: When students take my classes, they leave with their voice intact, she said.

I could circle but not touch the mind that had condemned Cyril Radcliffe to perpetual reincarnations as a bird, and I knew this was her right, even a possible imperative, to protect what MJ Thompson calls *the secret ministry commonly known as artistic practice.*

We came closest to the flint spark of contact when she told me that some viewers ran their hand along the pencil crayon banner of *Southall: Childplay*, and the residue had already damaged the print.

I'd like to hear your thoughts on that, I said, because from what I've seen, people touch art from an impulse of praise. They're moved to touch it. I know it can be harmful, but does it ever feel good?

She looked at me like someone who had worked for tens of thousands of hours on making beautiful objects. Who relied, for a livelihood, on their exhibition and sale.

I don't like it, she said.

An antique trolley toured our city in the summer, emitting its metallic narration, pausing at historical sites. Every round of passengers looked deflated at having paid too much. Driving is a method for not touching a place. Each day, a few passengers disembarked at the gallery.

Which way to the Rembrandts, they said. Or, We're here for the permanent collection. The European masters. They don't make them like that anymore, one man grinned.

It was in the tour pamphlet. Some visitors seemed to approach the idea of those paintings as they would a signature restaurant dish; they wanted to say, We ate the Rembrandts.

I didn't like them. That feeling was, I believe, a simplified equation of other feelings, where *x* was the dread of adults who could still be told what was important, where *y* was the suspicion that those people ran the world. I think the visitors may have worried that elitists like myself did: whoever had told them the Rembrandts mattered.

I tried to sort this out, stationed at the desk. The gallery's orienting principle was hospitality. Admission was free. Skateboarders were welcome on the outside ramp. In the summer, we propped the outer doors open to the sleepy campus, until a squirrel started to bring in walnuts and attempted to dig into the concrete floor of the entryway, as if to add a vault above our vaults. The bathrooms were open to everyone. It wasn't a setting where this hospitality was tested; we never had to ask, how long is too long to spend in a toilet stall, or, if a stroller is permitted in the galleries, why not a shopping cart? But I was aware that those potential situations wouldn't raise in me the friction I felt when I imagined people were looking at art wrong. Wrong meant admiring a painting for its bestowed value. It meant not really looking. I didn't know whether those visitors were or not; I was staring at the monitor again, at figures whose interior experiences were illegible. Viewing art is a subtractive skill, it takes curiosity, the release of defenses and pretensions—theirs and mine—letting the work charm or unsettle or shock us into presence. Allowing what we cannot touch to touch us.

Rembrandt didn't portray people in the masks of formal poses, but seemed to find them in the perishable instant, holding their figures in an empathetic gaze. The light is intimate, the brushstrokes are soft. To look is to adopt his vision as your own. If we count backwards through the generations—two parents, four grandparents, eight great-grandparents—then during the lives of Rembrandt and his models, our predecessors would number approximately half a million. A Milwaukee of ancestors. Through Rembrandt's paintings, we can feel deeply for someone who lived at that remove. Or maybe the salient part, for someone else, is the chestnut glow of a background, or a dropped knife hanging in the air like a feather.

At our gallery, I took one portrait as comforting evidence that even Rembrandt might have struggled with depicting hands, settling for one that resembles an inflated glove. When the painting was there, I mean; that summer, the Rembrandts were out on loan in Milwaukee. It was hardest to tell the few scholars who had made the trip specifically for his work, sometimes from overseas. I knew how to break bad news: be clear and kind, avoid euphemisms, affirm the listener's emotional response.

Then I'd encourage the disappointed guest to see the current exhibition, which was drawings, prints, paintings, and textiles by Northern Indigenous artists, largely from the 1970s; the second room included the Kenojuak Ashevak print. The alarm in that space kept going off inexplicably in the night, as if tripped by the motions of invisible creatures. I didn't mention that. Almost everyone who had sought us out for sixteenth-century portraiture emerged from the show quieted and brightened. The art had done its work.

We asked people to leave their drinks and collect them afterwards. Backpacks and large bags were also prohibited in the gallery. We offered to store everything in the enclosed area behind the desk because the lockers were unreliable. Once in a while, a visitor was indignant—my passport, will you take responsibility for that!? pointing a finger almost into me—though never anyone from demographics who might rightfully be tired of confiscations. To those wary of us we would recommend the lockers. They were automated, and each visitor entered their own four-digit code, which might later fail to open the locker. In a folder at the desk, we kept a lengthy master code, but it sometimes needed to be entered up to thirty times, though my own record was eleven.

The spirit of hospitality is to make the stranger feel at home. But every home has rules. The common linguistic root of the words *guest* and *host* signifies an ancient human practice of mutual obligations. I thought of the British arriving in India: how they would have been received, in many instances, with a hospitality they never intended to honour. Maybe what felt wrong to me, as I enacted an institutional version—in a setting that had for decades displayed colonially acquired objects—was that we operated on the assumption that everyone was a treacherous guest: our welcome was momentary but our surveillance constant.

I attended the opening of a group exhibit of paintings, ceramics, and jewelry at a commercial gallery. A festively dressed assortment of people crowded the room, and at the back was a table of tiny, architectural snacks. My friend was not there; her work had to speak for itself. She had hung clay flowers—invented, primordial, fungal—on a wall panel, and below them was a platform with their seedpods, petals, stamens. They were glazed with traces of colour and no two were the same. The wall component was not to be touched, but the platform pieces were different: PLEASE TAKE ONE, the sign read.

No way! Oh my god! That's incredible! I heard viewers say. Some had to be convinced by the curator. Then they picked up a ceramic flower part, turned it over, set it down. They were distinguishing the offerings by touch. Making the unpractised gesture of taking an item without, in both senses of the phrase, paying for it. They walked away, returned, changed their minds. The arrangement on the platform grew uneven; the chaos of others had entered the work. For the cottage! a woman said. Taking imbued a responsibility, which was part of the intention: What will you do with this seed that is fertile and fragile? Pods shown to friends, dropped into a pocket, wrapped in a napkin from the catering table. Another artist's ceramic plates, nearer to the entrance, were surrounded by signs that said Do Not Touch.

When I imagine ghosts, they are entities that see and hear, but don't make physical contact. Touch is for the living. Is our whole bodies. Closes the gap between lovers. Stays faithfully simultaneous, transmitting and receiving. Tells us unerringly whether the feeling is right or not, and when it's right, shakes us deeper than any other sense. It is the surface through which we may disappear momentarily into each other. How could it not be praise?

I returned to *When I grow up I want to be a namer of paint colours*. I wanted to see how others encountered the art. Monitoring them wasn't dull, like on the screens, because I was watching through the aperture of my own question. But I was there, and this defeated what I was after, although I tried to be unobtrusive as I studied the art and wrote in my notebook. People went quiet. Their privacy was gone, and they may have felt intimidated by what could be misinterpreted as expertise. This was the real robbery in art, the displacement of its open discussion into an exclusive realm.

I texted two friends who knew of my mission. Use your phone, one said, you'll seem distracted and normal. He was right. I didn't know my phone well; it probably had a notes app, but I couldn't find it, so I texted myself, every statement landing in duplicate. *Someone's phone rings with the old rotary ringtone. She silences it fast. She came from the room with* Hey Hey Paula, *the red rotary phone that never rings.*

At the marigold map, someone of South Asian background explains the history of partition to her white companion. Her hands flutter birdlike in front of her. Then two South Asian visitors look at the map. One reads the title to the other. They both laugh and the laughter says that they inherited this past. They look at the map for a long time. In another room, two people are speaking Punjabi about Punjabi.

The guards at this gallery patrol the spaces continuously. On my first day, the guard becomes someone to watch himself: sweaty, making his rounds with increasing speed and frequency, staring at people as if they are hallucinations. The next day the guard is familiar, someone I've seen in other years, and she has identified me as innocuous. I'm on a bench facing *the book of yellow*: four large books of handmade paper arranged on a dark wooden table.

Straw-like fibres burst from the page edges. Each spine lists yellow shades: *ambergris, Indian yellow, jaundice, mustard, turmeric*—the latter is also the colour of my skirt. To my right on the wall is *28 ambassador cars* featuring antique Volvo station wagons in bright colours, and for a while a girl in pyjamas printed with cartoon cars lingers in front of it.

An object, Stanley Eveling noted, *is a slow event.* These books were plants, pulp, paper; they were assembled, and they will disintegrate, but this current state of integrity is meant to last as long as possible. On the floor, half a metre or so in front of the table, a large text warning reads PLEASE DO NOT TOUCH THE ARTWORK, then a line of black tape, then a symbol of a hand crossed out. I watch three children take their positions carefully behind the line to view the books. One, leaning, loses her balance and steps over, says, Oh shit—the oldest quickly pulls her back. If your shoe is still touching the line, are you in or out?

Behind me is a large text piece that takes up a whole green wall, and the orange letters are made of clay. Children like to read it out loud. They sit facing the other way on the bench, jostling against my back. It is a good feeling, their comfortableness, their inability to be strangers. Some are so bored they rest their faces in their laps. A boy turns around and says, Hello! He is the only visitor who greets me in two days. One child, sounding out each word on the wall, keeps reading to the end, even when her teacher and classmates have moved on. Then it's quiet, except for the building's hum.

Another slow event begins. The guard stops at *the book of yellow*, radios someone. Ten minutes later, a colleague arrives, a taller figure. One of the books may have been moved. It's hard to say because their composition is irregular: two stacked, off kilter from each other, the third flat and elsewhere on the table, the fourth standing up. The tall guard repeats the work's title into his walkie-talkie. Then they both leave, and I feel compelled to stay and see what happens. Perhaps half an hour passes.

The two guards return and confer. I strain to listen. Someone has reviewed the video footage, and there is no evidence of anyone moving the books. But I could have sworn it was like this, the first guard says, and gestures with her hands. They cannot touch the art either. Then they leave again. People pass through the room in couples, in families, in groups, and I am starting to feel lonely. I want to know what happens with *the book of yellow*, but more than that I want to meet my friends for dinner.

On my way out, I detour past some favourite paintings. The guard is there, the familiar one, with short salt and pepper hair.

I ask if it happens particularly often, touching the art in the Dhaliwal show?

It happens in the whole gallery, she answers, every day. She walks me back to *the book of yellow* so we can look at it together. Shows me her favourite Dhaliwal piece, a painting of lush foliage and flowers with a toucan.

I ask, Why do you think people touch the art?

Yeah, she says, why do they!?

We're laughing and looking at *Outside the Zanzibar Tea Gardens*. I wait for more of an answer.

You know, she says, it is as if they've come to visit someone's house, and they're touching things without asking. That is bad manners!

Then she recommends her favourite restaurant to me.

Out the doors, the sauna of summer is cooking the pavements of Dundas Street. I hear a wailing that isn't human. Soon a fire truck rushes through, rightward like reading: the book of red, of dogwood, spider mite, cranberry, bindi, paprika, fiery mars. Its loudness has brought a thumping heartbeat to my throat. Brilliant vessel, slowing for the red light, determining that it means go.

DO NO HARM

I went to medical school in a prison town. At first, the prisons seemed to me like the sugar refineries or steel plants of other cities, a local industry on the periphery of my awareness. One of them was a grey, neoclassical, walled compound that loomed near the campus, against the lake. The prison across from the Value Village and Food Basics resembled a small castle with red spires; some called it Disneyland North. There were four other major institutions outside the city, less visible from the road.

Some students joked about them. Often they were young white men who, if they ever did find themselves in jail, would likely soon be freed through family connections, or a judge who saw himself reflected in their faces, their manner, their names. It was new for me to be around classmates like that—ones who might play a round of golf with the dean or department head, hired housekeepers, and shopped at thrift stores only satirically, at Halloween. In their company, the human rights activism I'd come to take for granted was considered amusing, though amusement was only the waxy coating over a compressed sense of entitlement; if I pushed through, I knew there would be contempt, even fury.

When it came to prisons, however, I had little to say; my circumstances had afforded me that ignorance. While my parents had modest incomes, they also had graduate degrees. The forms of racism I'd encountered were particular to being perceived as mixed, or South Asian, or Arabic; they were not anti-Black or anti-Indigenous, and therefore did not place me or my family at exponentially higher risk of imprisonment. I saw the prisons as ominous boxes, self-contained and arbitrarily situated in our area, and their relationship to the community remained obscure.

Then I volunteered for an after-school arts program at a local public school. I worked with first graders who had been labelled *at risk*. One afternoon, around a low, rectangular table strewn with pipe cleaners and popsicle sticks, one grim little girl in pigtails told me her father was a trucker and gone all the time. Immediately, two or three other children claimed the same.

When I raised this coincidence with their teacher afterwards, she clarified that the fathers were incarcerated. I can't recall what the teacher looked like, but I still hear her strike that tone the initiated might use to counter a privileged innocence: with a degree of pleasure at its erasure. In return, I made an effort to hide my dismay. And what do we do that for? I mean assimilate terrible facts by pretending not to feel.

What I had underestimated was the love in the lives of imprisoned people. I had pictured men—the downtown prison was a men's institution—without relations, and had failed to consider that their partners and children and mothers would move to live near them. It was my subtraction from their humanity. If my own father or brothers were prisoners, I too would try to make visits affordable and practical. That this situation seemed unimaginable was a new knowledge; I stood nearer to the fraternity men of my class than I had realized.

That sense of immunity was also undergoing an adjustment. It was 2001, and on September 11, during a break between our first and second lectures, a fellow student appeared at the lectern and said she had read at the library's computer terminal that America was under attack. The professor took the stage without comment, and the title of his PowerPoint presentation appeared on the screen: *Blood*. I listened for a few minutes, saw that the material was familiar, and left to get the news. In the months and years after, as an anti-terrorist infrastructure took shape, I would learn to be concerned for my brothers and their possible incarceration. I would grasp that, for whole classes of people, prison gates were only a crooked official or bureaucratic error away.

At that elementary school, however, the aches of reticent six-year-olds were still a revelation. Later, when I passed the prison, I could almost see their love and longing and anger for their fathers, tethered and drifting from the razor-wired walls like threads of spider silk.

The subsequent impression that the prisons made on me was an indirect but gruesome one. As part of our medical training, students were each required to shadow a paramedic team for one shift. I told my friend and classmate that I had spent a quiet evening eating doughnuts and watching comedies at the station. There was a single call from a woman with back pain, and the paramedics were relaxed as she limped from her house to the ambulance; she was a regular, they said. Then I asked my friend about his experience.

He was usually wryly funny, but now he explained that his team had been called to one of the prisons after a suicide. They had to cut a hanging man down. I felt for my friend, for the shock of the image he had absorbed and would have to live with. His voice was both incredulous and already imbued with a determined acceptance. I saw him steeling himself to demonstrate that he could withstand what he had witnessed.

Then came the clinical years.

I have lunch at twelve, a tall, thin patient in the infectious disease clinic told me. He repeated this several times as I persisted in a thorough assessment.

You're meeting someone for lunch? I asked.

No, he said, looking at me with scorn, I'm in prison.

The placid man in the waiting room—his partner or friend, I had assumed—must have been a guard.

The term minimum security occurred to me. The question of what he had done. *Never ask them that* was the only instruction I ever heard from a professor regarding prisoner patients.

As hospital admissions, prisoners were marked with a middle initial of X on our lists. This may have been to alert health-care workers to potential complications: the impossibility of a neurological exam on a person in shackles or the need to allow a guard into the imaging room. It seemed an invasive place to mark the difference, embedded in their names. The prisoner in-patients were people twice institutionalized. I wondered if the hospital was a respite for them.

One night I was called to a ward room with two uniformed guards at its door. There were four patients inside—three in the usual half-curtained beds, and one on a gurney in the aisle. I had his chart in my hands. Restraints locked his wrists and ankles to the rails, and were impossible to reconcile with his condition: he was emaciated, fevered, and trembling. He had multiple diagnoses, and his bloodwork indicated that he was critically ill.

I'm all right, he kept telling me in a small voice fractured with pain. I think it's just a cold.

We were approximately the same age. He had big, dark eyes. I told myself he had probably been violent, and that I had to stay alert to being tricked. I did that, I now see, to convince myself that his restraints made sense, that the system I was part of had its reasons—even if he was sick and couldn't turn on his side, or reach for water, or wipe sweat from his face. The vulnerability I perceived in him made me want to stay and hold his hand, but I knew to suppress this impulse. I was not there as a companion through this patient's harsh experience; the subtraction from his humanity was expected of me.

The following prisoner I remember was a bearded, red-haired man lying in a hallway on a gurney, handcuffed to its rails, awaiting surgery. It was another incongruous picture: pre-operative patients already seemed disarmed—they lacked their usual clothing, their glasses, their wedding rings, their sense of remove from their own mortality. The man's restraints, in this context, seemed to imply that the threat he posed was immense.

Immobilized by chains, he would be further paralysed by anaesthesia, then cut and cauterized and stitched. The meanings of these procedures blurred, and the rituals of surgery suddenly seemed potentially punitive, or even curative of whatever was amiss in him, an ablation of the will to harm.

These momentary images of corrective procedures now strike me as shadows of the carceral system's central and unsettled question: Should inmates be punished or rehabilitated? Isolation is already inherently painful to our nature. Past that punishing aspect, the condition of people released from prisons depends on the substance of their days, months, and years of imprisonment.

A doctor at one of the clinics I rotated through also worked inside the prisons. When I asked about his experience, he told me how disastrous it was that prisoners couldn't clean their needles for drug use. He had advocated for bleach buckets on the range, the common area directly outside the cells, but those were deemed too dangerous. Then he described a horrific economy in which some prisoners would swallow medications under supervision and later make themselves vomit to sell the pills. He seemed to speak with an extinguished kindness, in a sandpaper voice.

Contemporary prisons are supposed to have classrooms and libraries and culturally oriented anger management programs, measures intended to lead to the release of benign and skilled individuals. But what I've observed of people on day parole, on statutory release, or in resumed lives of relative freedom, is that living in prison leaves signs of trauma: scars, restlessness, a vigilant scanning of the periphery. Correctional officers, too, are affected by the institutional culture; a recent Canadian study found that more than a third suffer from work-related PTSD. When human exchanges are fraught with threat, everyone involved absorbs the fallout.

The historic downtown prison closed in 2013, and three years later it reopened for tourism. I visited on a bright day in May, a decade after I had left both the hospital and medicine itself; I wanted to know what was inside the walls I had passed by hundreds of times.

We gathered in the family visiting room; when it was in use, we were told, each round table had held a hidden surveillance microphone. Then the two college student guides led our group through tunneling hallways, into the domed space lined with tiered rows of cells. Under the dome was a panoptical guard station, a geometric structure of steel and bulletproof glass. Framed pictures hung on an outer wall: one photograph from the 1970s show inmates relaxed and crowded along the galleries, listening to a live concert. We saw the workshops where prisoners had manufactured goods for a fraction of minimum wage. Down one wing were a few open cells that we were permitted to enter.

At each stop, retired penitentiary officers told us the history of what we were viewing. Some seemed to offer a straightforward perspective. One former guard with a booming voice recalled the period when officer weapons were stored beneath the central guard station: Having the armoury here was wonderful. We could get anything we needed. Pistols, guns, gas, batons, shields.

A stern woman described doing cell checks: We looked for a live, breathing body.

Other narrators used forms of doublespeak I couldn't quite decipher. A gaunt man with a mustache said smilingly, When we got the security cameras, the prisoners really liked that.

The undesirables, others said. The definition of reasonable force.

The tour was strictly timed; whenever I lingered to ask questions, one of the students would return and rush me through the tight and labyrinthine passages after the group.

I thought of Charles Dickens's description of the place in 1842, when he was travelling through eastern America and Canada. Of this prison, he wrote: *There is an admirable jail here, well and wisely governed, and excellently regulated, in every respect.* At the time, some inmates were children under the age of ten, routinely whipped for breaking rules that included not speaking or giggling.

What felt cumulative, during our hour and a half in the now dormant building, was the effect of endless cold, hard surfaces—metal, limestone, and concrete—ubiquitous in the floors, the walls, the bars, the railings, the seats, the tables, the bunks. Everything was made to withstand force or to be hosed down, but people had lived here—breathing bodies—and I saw no means for them to be even fleetingly at ease. The answer to the punishment or rehabilitation question was inherent in the furnishings themselves.

Even as we walked the extensive outdoor grounds, a sense of suffocation persisted in me. Where were the former prisoners' voices? Inside a cell in the segregation unit, where a residual atmosphere of suffering was unmistakable, a charcoal drawing of an Indigenous Medicine Wheel, along with axes, a feather, and a grieving woman's face, still covered the cinderblock wall.

We were not supposed to ask, at the hospital, what a prisoner had done, because the answer could affect our duty to provide impartial care. This is a beautiful principle in medicine: the idea that every wound deserves the same quality of attention, no matter who bears it. But what if we had been asked, even once during a four-year curriculum, where injuries begin? With a famine; a slave ship; a broken treaty; the Sixties Scoop.

Some months after the tour, I was in a sharing circle at a community gathering. One of those present was a muscular white man with a tense demeanour. He volunteered that he had done what he called the worst thing possible, and had served his time, and was frustrated that many people—potential employers, friends, or lovers—still saw him as a criminal.

What about forgiveness? he asked.

He was sitting beside me, and we were without the separations that institutions impose—the white coat and the orange jumpsuit, the scripted roles of authority and compliance. He was speaking with a volatile impatience. Ideologically, I wanted to agree with his perspective, to erase the weight of his past, but instinctively, I wanted to be less near him, and I omitted from my own narrative the fact that I had a daughter. The fault wasn't mine or his, but collective; my sense, bodily and trusted, was that whatever had happened to him in the name of justice and rehabilitation had not worked. I don't believe prisons enclose or remediate physically violent behaviour. They are a stopover in its circuits, where pain and trauma are amplified.

Since the years that I was a student, activist movements for prison reform or abolition have grown in prominence. To envision new concepts of criminality, reparations, and sentences is to ask questions that start with language itself; for one thing, is what constitutes violence? At the after-school arts program, many of the children gathered around that glue-stained crafting table—who aren't children now, who probably have children of their own—were chronically hungry. To be six years old and hungry in a city of stocked stores, among gleaming billboard images of restaurant meals, is violence; to be a mother with only a few dollars of grocery money per day is violence; for a child to name their hunger to the wrong adult and lose their family is violence. And then there is that quieter inflicting on ourselves, when we work in institutions, the numbing that allows us to withstand how the system functions.

In relation to countless pervasive forms of violence, most of us accord ourselves a false sense of blamelessness. We don't lower the rates of social assistance programs, or close the supervised injection site, or fasten the handcuffs to the stretcher. Our violence takes the form of silent, continuous consent; it lives in us, a negative space with armoured walls.

After the prison tour, I remembered another way the subject of the prisons had been mentioned when I was still getting to know my medical school classmates: the downtown penitentiary was rumoured to house Paul Bernardo, a serial rapist who also murdered three girls. My cohort was the same generation as his teenage victims, and it was natural that we would discuss him—but now I also see the implications of us naming only that single inmate, one who was monstrous and undoubtedly guilty and could never be safely released. Very few such people exist, but it was convenient to consider him the representative prisoner because it absolved us of asking who else was in there, and what their stories might be. Stories in which we are all complicit, because those hard and unforgiving surfaces are ours.

AFTER ETTY

The room I rent in Amsterdam is up three steep and creaking flights of stairs. Its desk holds an electric kettle, a catalogue of tea bags in a tin, dark rye slices in cellophane, packets of spreadable yellow cheese, two USB ports, and brochures: canal tours, the Heineken Experience, and the Anne Frank House, a place I haven't found the capacity to witness—too implosive of the heart, her wide smile of teeth still sharp with newness. Anne Frank copied into her diary a sentence by F. de Clercq-Zubli: *In a true book, the writer writes himself free.* The book in my bag is like that. I'm here for the ghost of its writer, another young and sanguine person who kept a diary during the war and was killed in a Nazi camp.

Esther Hillesum was in her mid-twenties when the war began. After law school, she had started to study psychology and Slavic languages. Hillesum was bright and moody and charming, and she dreamt of practicing Jungian therapy, of seeing Russia, her mother's birthplace, and of becoming a novelist—*later,* she wrote, *when I will really write.*

I leave my room to look for her old house. On the Museumplein, tourists are sitting on the pond's ledge, taking pictures. I am navigating by Hillesum's description of the view from the home where she boarded: *The red and the white tulip bud, inclined toward each other, the noble grand piano, black and mysterious and complicated, a being in itself, and behind the windows the black branches against the light sky and further still the Rijksmuseum.* The meander of her sentences is in my notebooks and my mind; I am studying her journals, which read so intimately that her name to me is Etty, as it was to family and friends.

When I was eighteen or nineteen, I read the abridged version of Etty's journals unevenly, taking eager instruction from her unconventional sexuality, skipping the passages on God and prayer—I'd already strayed from the Islamic and Christian traditions I was raised in—and almost devotionally assimilating her perspectives on writing. Now I am ten years older than Etty was when she died, and writing and sex are still compelling, but I'm no longer averse to contemplating spirituality. Reading the comprehensive edition of her journals and letters, I allow lines to percolate, absorb incongruities, and follow flurries of references. At home, her words and ideas live in me as I do the laundry, or shovel snow, or wait in the lineup at the grocery store. Muslims refer to adherents of Christianity and Judaism as the people of the book, and have their own poetic text, but Etty's heavy volume is the closest I've come to a book I have faith in. I've heard others confide, though only rarely, a text of similar significance to them: *A Room of One's Own, Anna Karenina, Beloved.*

Etty's voice is searching and intelligent and sentient, amusing and confiding, and balanced somehow as she reviews her romances and friendships, reads Dostoevsky, wrestles with the pregnancy she doesn't want, praises an apple tart, jasmine blossoming in an alley, the shape of a lover's mouth. Etty was after what she called her *oerbron*, primal source, and affirmed or admonished her own progress with playful sternness, often writing in direct address to *that very deepest in me, that for the sake of ease I call God.* Etty is obscure and universal—almost no one in my circles knows of her, but her journal has been published in eighteen translations. In part because I am not reading one of those, because her words are in my mother tongue, I swallow them like milk.

On the eve of the Dutch surrender to the Nazis, Etty was at her desk when she spotted one of her former professors on what is now the Museumplein. His name was Bonger.

That image, that lumbering figure with the head lifted sideways to the smoke clouds in the distance, I will never forget, she wrote. Etty had gone out to speak to him, taking his arm as they walked. She asked what he made of people's attempts to flee to England, and whether he thought democracy would prevail. It would certainly prevail, he predicted, but its restoration would take several generations. He was a prominent criminologist and a blustering lecturer; now he seemed deflated. He thanked her for walking with him. The next day she visited a friend's home and heard that Bonger had shot himself perhaps an hour after their encounter.

I'm at the far end the square. My nerves hum. This has to be the Gabriel Metsustraat, and its houses are few. Nearing their tight row, I find a small plaque beside a door: *In this house ETTY HILLESUM wrote her diaries 1941–1942.* I place my palm on its red stone. A pulse that is mine but seems embedded in the wall. One floor up, in the window of her old room—where there had been a table with a fringed cloth, Russian grammar exercises, spring crocuses in an old tin, a cup of coffee while there was coffee, Rilke's works, slit envelopes, where Etty wrote hundreds of pages meant for her alone until she knew that she wouldn't survive and gave them to friends to publish—looming in that window is the steel range hood of an expensive kitchen.

Etty struggled during visits to her parents' home: *It is depressing. It is tragi-comic, I don't know what kind of crazy household this is, but a person cannot flourish here.* In a 1931 family portrait, her father Louis is pulled back in his chair as if in silent opposition to the scene. Etty's mother, Rebecca, who fled Russia after a pogrom, appears formidable and tense. The youngest child, Mischa, brings them together, one arm around his mother and the other on his father's knee. Middle brother Jaap is in the background in small glasses and a suit. Etty, in a flowing dress, gives the camera a pensive, scrutinizing look. All her portraits seem to fuse an inwardness with an awareness of performance.

Jaap studied medicine in Amsterdam during the same years Etty was there, and Mischa, who lived with their parents, was a virtuosic pianist and composer. Both were hospitalized at various times for psychiatric conditions, and Etty herself had recurrent depressions, exhaustions, and migraines. In 1941, a friend convinced her to visit the psychochirologist Julius Spier.

Spier was Jewish and a refugee from early Nazism in Berlin. He was fifty-four years old, divorced, the father of two grown children. After a business career, he had studied psychology in Zurich with Carl Jung. He had a fiancée in London.

At his sessions, Spier would invite his students and followers to observe him as he read the palms of a volunteer subject. In Etty's hands, he saw philosophical and intuitive gifts. Spier's techniques were at odds with the ethics of psychotherapy. At Etty's first private consultation, for example, he wrestled her into submission in order to measure her physical powers. During the session that followed, he suggested that she give him *a little friendship kiss*, and at a subsequent one asked, *Did you think of me this week? To be honest, I thought of you a great deal.*

Etty soon became Spier's friend, student, secretary, and lover. He kept a number of other female admirers close. Etty was sexually adventurous. She explored making love with Spier and a friend at the same time, and, prior to and throughout her involvement with him, also enjoyed a relationship with the landlord at her boarding house.

As a teenager, I stared at Spier's photograph and couldn't understand Etty's passion. On this second reading, I feel pulled between concern for her susceptibility to his exploitation, and envy at the depth of their contact. We often only realize belatedly that someone with power took advantage of us, and Etty never had that longer retrospect. During the two and a half years of her writings, Spier appears first as a figure of infatuation, then a transformative companion, and after his death from lung disease, a presence Etty recalls with love.

The journals began as homework that Spier assigned. Hanneke Starreveld, a friend of Etty's, said he encouraged all his clients to keep a notebook to express *the innermost material that could be converted into words.* Etty started hers a month after meeting him, reluctantly, in writing that her friends would later find laborious to decipher: *Great inhibitions, I don't dare to give things away, to let them flow out of me freely, and yet will have to, should I wish in due course to bring life to a reasonable and satisfactory end.*

On the Waterlooplein, while waiting for the Jewish Historical Museum to open, I sip a lukewarm coffee. It is 2017, and if Etty were alive, she would be 103 years old. I imagine her, at the edge of temporal possibility, as a diminutive figure in a belted dress, shoes somewhere between sensible and stylish, watching her city from a wheelchair parked in the sun.

The journals are untouchable under glass: five of the nine found notebooks, thin and spiral-bound, with stained, worn covers of dull blue, grey, maroon, and ochre. One is open, revealing a hurried cursive in which many syllables, and some entire words have been denoted simply as flat lines. A private, almost coded script.

Hanging beside the journals is a roll of faded fabric, printed with a grid of the word *Jood* in Stars of David, each bordered by a dotted cutting line. That public marking of the Jewish people started during an interval for which the corresponding notebook, number seven, hasn't been found. Even if it was, the *Jodensterren* might be absent from its pages. In Etty's early journals, her attention is inward and otherwise on her immediate community, and the occupation appears only intermittently, like a wind that blows a door open and then shut: a boy has fallen from a plane, a friend needs help preparing his backpack for the night train to incarceration.

For an interval, Etty was protected by unusual freedoms. She worked for a group called the Jewish Council, which meant that while others were receiving their summons for Westerbork concentration camp, she held a pass that allowed her to travel between the camp and home, functioning as a kind of social worker. At Westerbork one night, sleeping women and girls surrounded Etty in three-level bunks. She had heard them lament during the day that they no longer wanted to think or feel, or they would go mad, and Etty prayed: *Then let me be the thinking heart of these barracks.*

The journals take a gradual turn from introversion to what Etty called the chronicling of her time. But even when early wartime events crossed her mind, she conveyed them with distinctive clarity. For example, I knew that the German occupiers eventually banned Jewish people from riding bicycles. I had absorbed that fact in its plainest form, a class of people without bikes, but it was through Etty's words that I came to follow it through to its consequences: hours of walking, strengthened muscles, open blisters, exhaustion, shoe soles that wore out and could not be replaced. And when Etty does mention the Star of David badge, after meeting her youngest brother at a streetcar stop, the image is unforgettable: *That yellow star fluttered shabbily and with frayed edges on his grey, not too clean, open raincoat, and he waved his heavy suitcase back and forth and had such a cheerful, sweet face: Mischa.*

In Amsterdam, Café Wildschut is the starting point for a walking tour of Etty Hillesum's neighbourhoods. I'm the only registrant. The guide waves over the crowded patio with a shy flourish and says, This is where Etty and her friends celebrated her graduation from the Faculty of Law.

We move through the contemporary city—the pavements alive with beer drinkers gathered around cast-iron tables, and small children riding on the front of their mothers' bicycles, and construction crews jackhammering at ancient sewers—an almost hallucinating pair, picturing the years when the Apollobuurt was housing for Jewish German refugees, and the synagogue was shut, and a local high school was the headquarters of the Nazi Sicherheitsdienst.

The tour concludes with a finely researched revelation; we're at the Stadionkade, and the guide points out a bench. This is where Etty Hillesum and Julius Spier would have sat together, he tells me—he has checked the city archives for the age of the bench and the absence of other seating there in the 1940s.

I sit in that phantom space alone as the warmth evaporates from the day. Time curls like incense smoke. Two ducks swim along a canal that is lined with docked houseboats. The neighbourhood seems prosperous and calm. I can sense that history has already shifted its weight since I was a child.

Anyone over forty had been alive during the war then. My older cousins were still subject to conscription, and my mother and aunts and uncles stored big sacks of potatoes, carrots, and onions under the stairs. War is what we often played out in the streets. We chose allied countries on both sides; no one wanted to be Nazis. Occasionally, a car with white plates—German—would pass through our neighbourhood, and we would chase after it. That's hard to picture now. The witnessed war lives in nursing homes; soon, what happened may still be commemorated, but it will not be recalled.

Westerbork has been, throughout its history, a place of stunning incongruity. It was founded by the Dutch government in 1939 as a refugee camp for Jewish Germans fleeing to the Netherlands; those refugees became inmates when the Nazis took over the following year. After the war, the enclosure was used as a prison for Dutch Nazi collaborators, initially guarded by the remaining Jewish residents. Subsequently, the camp became a training centre for Dutch soldiers sent to repress the independence movement in Indonesia, and finally it was used to house refugee Indonesians who had fought for the colonial army but were then refused Dutch citizenship.

During Etty's months there, Westerbork was a transit camp for Auschwitz and other extermination sites, and therefore had two irreconcilable purposes. It was meant first of all to prevent panic or mutiny among the detainees, and dispel within the wider Dutch population the rumours of death camps. To this end, there was generally enough to eat. Residents were allowed to send innocuous mail and to receive care packages. There was a school, a synagogue, a theatre, and a hospital equipped to do surgeries. Because many excellent doctors were Jewish, it was among the best hospitals in the country.

At the same time, once a week at midnight, the camp commandant would distribute a list of resident names, up to several thousand, who would be forced within hours to board a train to Poland. Every day, the people in the camp scrambled and negotiated to have themselves and their loved ones placed on other lists of exceptions or deferrals. At any moment, the lists that were presumed to be safe could collapse and be added to the transport list. The destination was supposed to be a labour camp, but no one could fail to notice that some transports consisted largely of the sick, the elderly, and the very young.

This is where Etty chose to stay when her travel privileges ran out. Friends begged her to go into hiding instead, even attempting to kidnap her and take her to a rural location. She told them, You don't understand me, I want to share the fate of my people.

Mischa also turned down a possible means of survival. The Nazis had granted him exceptional status, in recognition of his musical accomplishments, which meant he could be interned with other prominent Jewish people at a rural estate. He declined because his parents were not exempted, and in response the three of them were immediately sent to Westerbork. Etty was already at the camp and wrote to a friend that the day of their arrival was the blackest of her life.

Where was God is a question some people have felt confronted with when considering the Nazi extermination camps and other twentieth-century disasters: Where was the intervention of the omnipotent being, or where was mercy? In the journals, Etty's God is not almighty but internal and elusive, vulnerable to getting lost. She writes: *This becomes steadily clearer to me, that you cannot help us, but that we have to help you and through that we help ourselves. And this is the only thing that we can save in this time and also the only thing that matters: a piece of you in ourselves, God.* Perhaps her answer later would have been that God—whom she describes also as *the beautiful and immense feeling for this life that I have within me*—could be present only while people protected that capacity inside themselves. She wanted that God to exist in the camp.

Etty, along with her parents and Mischa, was on the transport list on September 7, 1943. Her last known correspondence is a postcard that she pushed through an opening in the train car while they were still in the Netherlands. It was found by a farmer and mailed. None of the Hillesums survived the war. Etty was killed at Auschwitz on November 30th, the specific cause of her death unknown.

I am drawn to Etty's concept of god. I find, as I read her, that a sense of faith, unbidden and amorphous, persists unexpectedly somewhere in me. But the void of her last months, without diaries or letters, disturbs that little pilot light. I can't know if her theology worked under the worst conditions—and isn't that required for belief? And then, slowly, listening to the radio news, doing dishes, tucking my child into bed, that expectation starts to unravel. I want something unbreakable, but on this earth, I can't have it. Dutch poet Lucebert's famous line, written decades after the war, comes back to me often: *Everything of value is defenseless.* What if god might be flowering or drowning inside of us, on any given afternoon. What if the inner gesture for holding god is similar to how we lift a robin's fractured eggshell from the grass. What if we sometimes have to breathe god back into each other. And if we die during an interval when god is missing, what if that isn't failure but circumstance; one for which we deserve to be held.

From Amsterdam, I take an eastbound train. I've seen examples of the summons documents for Westerbork, stamped with a date and time, often in the night, to appear at the Centraal Station, and a list of the luggage one was allowed to bring, including one spoon, one mug, and two pairs of socks.

I stop at Deventer, where Etty's parents lived. *In Deventer,* Etty wrote, *there were grain fields, that I will never forget and where I almost kneeled down, there was the IJssel with the colourful parasol and the straw roof and the patient horses. And then, the sun, that I let in through all pores.*

Soon I'm at the IJssel River, and unlike in Amsterdam, where picturing the wartime city means blotting out the crowded, digital present, here the exercise is effortless. The river's body follows the same curves. Jackdaws and terns sweep over the banks; the air smells of mown grass and mud. A slow barge ploughs a passing furrow in the waves, and church bells ring softly, slowly, rurally.

The Etty Hillesum Centrum is in a former synagogue and Jewish school. Inside the modest space are two permanent exhibits, one on Deventer's Jewish history and one on Etty's life and work. A bronze bust, made after her death by a friend who tried to picture Etty at Auschwitz, shows her emaciated hand symbolically holding a pen. A room of paintings depicts Etty's erotic relationship with Julius Spier. A volunteer explains that the Centrum also educates hundreds of school children annually on xenophobia and racism in the Netherlands, and is a registered reporting centre for victims or witnesses of discrimination.

Hearing that my former country is starting to name racism has both satisfying and melancholy elements: at last, so late—this too has changed since I was a girl. I climb the stairs to the narrow loft with the archive, and settle in with my notebooks. The volunteer brings me coffee and gingerbread.

The range of materials is remarkable—filmed interviews with Etty's aged friends, the self-published work of a woman who believes herself to have been Etty in a past life, hundreds of popular and scholarly analyses, as well as artistic responses that Etty's work inspired.

The interview footage both heightens and alters Etty's reality to me. Here are two of her friends, both presences in the journals: they have grown old, escaped from the bell jar world of the book into reality. Their accents are strikingly upper class, and I am startled to consider that Etty, of the confiding, earthy writing voice, may have sounded like that. My idea of her absorbs new facts: Etty was shy about going to parties alone, she addressed her friends with invented endearments, and they didn't know of her relationship with her landlord, or of her religious faith.

I go on to Westerbork. The countryside is green and scattered with small villages, but closer to the former camp the landscape turns to heath and pines. Later, the son of a nearby farmer will tell me that his father was able hear the wartime trains at night. If the sound continued in the familiar manner, the train was heading to the city; if it quieted unusually, then it had taken the new bend into the concentration camp.

At the Westerbork museum, over displays of suitcases and shoes, speakers play a recording of Etty's writings. The camp itself is deeper into the woods, and the trail features an independent exhibit: a scale model of the solar system, in which each step represents approximately 2.5 million kilometres. I do sense a gravitational pull: this place will be the culmination of my search, and I long for it to bring the ghost of Etty closer, and feel the heaviness of nearing the site where a hundred thousand people were imprisoned and sent to their deaths.

The solar system trail ends at the Westerbork Synthesis Radio Telescope, a wide, fenced strip of land that contains a row of enormous satellite dishes. The instruments are located here because of the relative absence of cell and radio signals. I pause under the pines to watch the concave instruments, massive and receptive, the air above them shimmering with summer warmth. I wonder what they've heard. *And then listening, listening everywhere,* Etty wrote as instruction to herself, *listening to the very ground of things.*

The rustic villa of the camp commandant, outside the Westerbork gates, stands enclosed in a glass and steel structure. Sunlight gleams and refracts from the exterior, and is of the present, while the wooden building within, with its flaking green and white paint, seems trapped in an airless past.

The dry grass crunches under my feet. The camp is largely empty, its buildings and facilities dismantled, the old foundations overgrown. I approach what remains of the train. More than seventy people were forced into each cargo car, sharing one barrel of drinking water and one barrel for excrement. I knew this, but had unthinkingly pictured a modern boxcar. The difference is only a detail, but when I see the two old freight cars of maroon wood, small and low, impossible for seventy people to occupy, the cold wind of the past sweeps through me. The camp's culture must have been one of desperation, dissociation, and terror.

Etty's days here started with collecting a thermos from each of her parents, who were in separate barracks, and waiting in line for hot water to bring them tea. Then she checked on Mischa. She consoled patients in the sick barracks and sat by the beds of injured inmates shipped from the prison camps of Amersfoort and Vught. At night she sometimes stood at the registration tables to orient and comfort newly captured families.

In a letter smuggled past the censors, Etty recounts the following:

> I sat on a summer night, eating my red cabbage at the edge of that yellow lupine field, that stretched from our food barracks to the delousing barracks, and mused pensively, inspired: "One ought to write the Chronicle of Westerbork." An older man at my side—likewise with red cabbage—answered: "Yes, but then one would have to be a great poet."
>
> He is right, one would have to be a great poet, journalistic stories will no longer do.

Etty befriended a journalist, Philip Mechanicus, who was also imprisoned at Westerbork. He would read to her his detailed notes on life in the camp. In their book form, a three-hundred-page volume, Mechanicus' voice is one of eloquent, sardonic resignation, observing people as if he is watching a film.

He is a writer using bleak humour because the alternative is collapse. Reading him, I feel steeped in despair, and without Etty's example I would have believed this to be inevitable in narratives of concentration camps. But her descriptions make me feel something closer to a sense of awe. Against Etty's account of a transport night, written to friends in August 1943, her journal seems like rehearsal; at Westerbork, she found her material, and gave it brilliant, authentic, and devastating form.

That letter and one other were clandestinely published as a pamphlet during the war, under a disguised title: *Three letters from the painter Johannes Baptiste van der Pluym (1843–1912)*. Etty describes the case of a boy who is shocked to appear on the deportation list and, in a moment of bewilderment, hides in a tent. His fellow inmates are sent to hunt for him, on the commandant's threat to send fifty others to Auschwitz in his place, including his closest friends. The boy is soon found, but then the fifty additional people have to go after all, as a deterrent to hiding. Etty writes of a partially paralysed girl, learning to walk again, who has to get on the train and declines to take a plate, saying she knows that she will die in Poland, and then the Germans will have a plate. She writes of pressing tomato juice to fill bottles for wailing babies. Of a stately old woman whose husband has recently died, remarking that the Germans will not even let her go to the grave beside him. Of the commandant—a man who loved attending performances at the camp's theatre—unhurriedly riding his bicycle along the train for a final inspection, and of the hands waving family and friends goodbye through the cracks in the wagons, and of the laughter of the armed guards.

Let me be the thinking heart of these barracks. Writing is a translation of our attention, and Etty's possessed such presence that even within a nightmare she could see a world. When she later wrote to a friend that she still found life in its depths to be wondrously good, she was not speaking from a refusal to acknowledge its horrors, but from an almost incomprehensibly holistic vision.

At the former camp, a tour bus has unloaded. I join their guided walk. People are wearing T-shirts with English slogans, loosened earbuds, blank expressions. I overhear travelers from Israel and Iran.

We do not have to know each other under duress; we only have to behave as groups of strangers do in such a setting, standing not too close together, agreeing that the day is warm. Etty wrote that here, she learned to decipher people, to read life down to its innermost skeleton—but we remain largely inscrutable to one another because although there are refugees drowning in the Mediterranean, and anti-Islamists seated in the Dutch parliament, and white supremacists marching in America, in an immediate sense there's nothing wrong.

We look at the restored frame of a barracks, and at the old railway tracks, which are now a monument, the ends pulled up so that they curve jaggedly into the sky. Anne Frank and her parents and sister passed through here after their capture, the guide reminds us.

As our tour group dissembles, the next one arrives. I have a few sprigs of heather that I meant to leave for Etty, to thank her for finding the words. I search for her presence, under the clusters of pine and beech trees, along the sand embankments, through the spectral walls of former barracks, but she seems not to be there at all. Lupins still grow everywhere, past blooming, gone to seed. All I can do is fill my pockets with the dark and rustling pods, to plant when I get home.

ACKNOWLEDGEMENTS

'Found' is for Steven Heighton, who looked for the notebook on his runs. Earlier versions of these essays appeared in *The New Quarterly*, *Geist*, *The Malahat Review*, and *Brick*. 'Spirit Materials' was included in *Sharp Notions: Essays from the Stitching Life* (Arsenal Pulp Press, 2023) and 'Do No Harm' and 'Found' in the *Best Canadian Essays 2024* and *2025* editions respectively (Biblioasis). 'In The Field' was shortlisted for the 2022 Constance Rooke Creative Nonfiction Prize and 'The Singing Bone' won third place in the 2021 Edna Staebler Personal Essay Contest. I'm grateful to Pamela Mulloy, Marita Dachsel, Nancy Lee, Iain Higgins, Tanvi Bhatia, Laurie Graham, Allison LaSorda, Marcello Di Cintio, Emily Urquhart, Orly Zebak, and the other editors at these publications.

Deep thanks to Liz Johnston, who mended the sentences so astutely. To Kyo Maclear and Elamin Abdelmahmoud, faculty for the Banff Centre for the

Arts Literary Journalism session in 2024, and to the cohort of fellow writers. To all the Villanelles, for fifteen years of cheering and critique. To Aimee Dunn, whose Palimpsest Press is a wonder, and to cover designer Ellie Hastings and copy editor Ashley Van Elswyk. To Jim Johnstone, for lending this project his enthusiasm, intelligence, and patience. To Imaan Bayoumi, the late Kee Dewdney, Sarindar Dhaliwal, Pasha Malla, Paul Masiowski, Marney McDiarmid, Max Montalvo, Soraya Roberts, Amy Rubin, Judith Spitters, Anne-Marie Turza, and Lieke Weima, for the conversations. To Max, for the beautiful painting of the field. And to all my dear ones, thank you for making me possible.

This book was written with funding from the Canada Council for the Arts, the Ontario Arts Council, The Writers' Trust of Canada's Woodcock Fund, the Marian Hebb Research Grant, and York University's Writer-In-Residence Program.

NOTES

/// sources are listed in the order they occur in the essays
/// translations from Dutch are by the author unless otherwise noted

FOUND

Millet, Jean-François. *The Gleaners.* 1857, Musee d'Orsay, Paris.

Varda, Agnes. *The Gleaners and I.* Zeitgeist Films, 2002.

BLOODWORK

Baldwin, James. "The Artist's Struggle for Integrity." November 1962, Community Church, New York City. Speech.

Covey, Stephen R. *The 7 Habits of Highly Effective People: Restoring the Character Ethic.* Simon and Schuster, 1989.

Bishop, Elizabeth. "At The Fishhouses." *Poems,* edited by Saskia Hamilton, Farrar, Straus & Giroux, 2011, pp. 62-64.

Magritte, René. *The Lovers*. 1928, Museum of Modern Art, New York.

Cohen, Leonard. "A Kite Is A Victim." *The Spice-Box of Earth*. McClelland & Stewart, 1961, p. 1.

Paley, Grace. "The Art of Fiction No. 131."" Interview with Jonathan Dee, Barbara Jones, and Larissa MacFarquhar. *The Paris Review*, Issue 124, Fall 1992, pp. 181-209.

Stevenson, Anne. "The Spirit is too Blunt an Instrument." *The Collected Poems of Anne Stevenson, 1955–1995*. Oxford University Press, 1996.

Plath, Sylvia. *The Unabridged Journals of Sylvia Plath*, edited by Karen V. Kukil, Anchor Books, 2000, p. 328.

Foucault, Michel. *The Birth of the Clinic*. Routledge, 2003.

Carver, Raymond. "What the Doctor Said." *All of Us: The Collected Poems*. Harvill Press, 1996.

Vroman, Leo. "Mens." *Uit Slaapwandelen*. Querido, 1957.

Wright, James. "Lying in a Hammock at William Duffy's Farm in Pine Island, Minnesota." *Above the River: The Complete Poems and Selected Prose*. Wesleyan University Press, 1990.

Bishop, Elizabeth. "At The Fishhouses." *Poems*, edited by Saskia Hamilton, Farrar, Straus & Giroux, 2011, pp. 62-64.

IN THE FIELD

Kafka, Franz. *The Blue Octavo Notebooks*, edited by Max Brod. Translated by Ernst Kaiser and Eithne Wilkins, Exact Change, 1991.

DWAALLICHTJES

Hermans, W.F. *Nooit Meer Slapen.* De Bezige Bij, 2003, p. 99.

Rubinstein, Renate. "Het 4-mei-gevoel." *Amsterdam: Zestig liefdesverklaringen zwart op wit,* edited by Els de Jong, H.J.W. Becht, p. 81

Hall, Phil. *Killdeer.* BookThug, 2011, p. 11.

Penone, Giuseppe. *The Hidden Life Within.* Art Gallery of Ontario, October 2, 2011–February 6, 2012.

Van Gogh, Vincent. *De Aardappeleters.* 1885, Van Gogh Museum, Amsterdam.

Klei, A.J. *De Meeste Mensen Zijn Aardig.* Balans, 1991.

https://www.hetscheepvaartmuseum.nl/doen/de-schepen/voc-schip-amsterdam/denk-mee [text has changed]

Verheugen, Serge. *Buurtberoemd.* 2019, Muiderpoort Station, Amsterdam.

THE SINGING BONE

Rawie, Jean Pierre. "Ursa Minor II." *Maatstaf,* vol. 39, no. 3, 1991, p. 63.

Kranenburg Begraafplaats website [expired].

Grimm, Jacob and Wilhelm Grimm. *De Sprookjes van Grimm.* Translated by M.M. de Vries-Vogel, Het Spectrum, 1984.

Koff, Clea. *The Bone Woman: A Forensic Anthropologist's Search for Truth in the Mass Graves of Rwanda, Bosnia, Croatia, and Kosovo.* Random House, 2005.

The Bible: Authorized Version, edited by John Stirling, Oxford University Press, 1966, p. 681.

SPIRIT MATERIALS

Hockney, David. Interview with Michael Govan. *Interview Magazine*, November 5, 2013, pp. 120-127.

DRAWING LINES

Dhaliwal, Sarindar. *When I grow up I want to be a namer of paint colours.* July 23, 2023–July 14, 2024, Art Gallery of Ontario, Toronto.

Thompson, MJ. "The Colour of Childhood." *The Radcliffe Line and Other Geographies: Sarindar Dhaliwal,* edited by Marcie Bronson, Rodman Hall Art Centre/Brock University, The Reach Gallery Museum Abbotsford, The Robert McLaughlin Gallery, 2017, p. 63.

Matharu, Pamila and Rajni Perera. "Sarindar's Influence." *Foyer.* Art Gallery of Ontario, October 5, 2023, https://readfoyer.com/article/sarindars-influence. December 2, 2024.

Hillesum, Etty. *Het Werk*. Amsterdam, Balans, 2012, p. 25.

Matharu, Pamila and Rajni Perera. "Sarindar's Influence." *Foyer.* Art Gallery of Ontario, October 5, 2023, https://readfoyer.com/article/sarindars-influence December 2, 2024.

Ashevak, Kenojuak. *Owl of the Sea.* 1977, Agnes Etherington Art Centre, Kingston.

Hudson, Anna, et al. *Tunirrusiangit: Kenojuak Ashevak and Tim Pitsiulak*, edited by Anna Hudson, Jocelyn Piirainen, Georgianna Uhlyarik, Art Gallery of Ontario and Goose Lane Editions, 2018, p. 48.

Van Rijn, Rembrandt. *De Nachtwacht.* 1642, Rijksmuseum, Amsterdam.

Munro, Eleanor. *Originals: American Women Artists.* Simon & Schuster, 1979, p. 96.

Bernstein Sycamore, Mattilda. *Touching the Art.* Soft Skull Press, 2023, p. 81.

Thompson, MJ. "The Colour of Childhood." *The Radcliffe Line and Other Geographies: Sarindar Dhaliwal,* edited by Marcie Bronson. Rodman Hall Art Centre/Brock University, The Reach Gallery Museum Abbotsford, The Robert McLaughlin Gallery, 2017, p. 54.

Dhaliwal, Sarindar. Personal Interview. March 9–10, 2024.

Thompson, MJ. "The Colour of Childhood." *The Radcliffe Line and Other Geographies: Sarindar Dhaliwal,* edited by Marcie Bronson. Rodman Hall Art Centre/Brock University, The Reach Gallery Museum Abbotsford, The Robert McLaughlin Gallery, 2017, p. 53.

McDiarmid, Marney. "There was too much to hold it all" and "What's mine is yours." *New Dimensions 2024.* July 13–27 2024, Wall Space Gallery, Ottawa.

Kirshenblatt-Gimblett, Barbara. "Intangible heritage as metacultural production." *Museum International*, vol. 56, no. 1/2, May 2004, pp. 52-65.

DO NO HARM

Dickens, Charles. *American Notes for General Circulation.* Penguin Classics, 2001, ch. 15.

AFTER ETTY

de Clercq-Zubli, Frida. "Anne's Book of Beautiful Sentences." *Annefrank.org*, 28 December 2024, https://www.annefrank.org/en/anne-frank/diary/annes-book-of-beautiful-sentences/.

Hillesum, Etty. *Het Werk*. Amsterdam, Balans, 2012, p. 300.

Het Werk, p. 309.

Het Werk, p. 523.

Het Werk, p. 55.

Het Werk. p. 85.

Het Werk, p. 48.

Het Werk, p. 49.

Johanna Smelik en Hanneke Starreveld vertellen over Etty. Etty Hillesum Centrum, 1998. DVD.

Het Werk, p. 4.

Het Werk, p. 575.

Het Werk, p. 398.

Het Werk, p. 792.

Het Werk, p. 516.

Het Werk, p. 527.

Lucebert. *Verzamelde Gedichten*. Amsterdam, De Bezige Bij, 2002.

Het Werk, p. 72.

Het Werk, p. 286.
Het Werk, p. 255.
Mechanicus, Philip. *In Depot: dagboek uit Westerbork.* Verbum, 2008.
Hillesum, Etty. *Drie brieven van den kunstschilder Johannes Baptiste van der Pluym (1843–1912): met twee reproducties, uitgegeven en van een toelichting voorzien door A.C.G. Botterman-v.d. Pluym.* Haarlem, 1943.
Het Werk, p. 575.

PHOTO CREDIT: MAX MONTALVO

Sadiqa de Meijer is the author of *Leaving Howe Island* (2013 finalist for the Governor General's Award in Poetry), *The Outer Wards* (2020), and *alfabet/alphabet* (2020 winner of the Governor General's Award in Non-Fiction). Her writing also appears in *Brick*, *The Walrus*, *LitHub*, *Poetry*, *Poetry London*, and other venues. She lives in Katarokwi/Kingston, Ontario, where she is currently Poet Laureate.